Understanding Broadcast Journalism

Understanding Broadcast Journalism presents an insightful exploration of broadcast journalism today; its characteristics, motivations, methods and paradigms. The authors balance discussions of industry practice with critical examinations of content, across television, radio and associated multiplatform journalism. They highlight key issues including ownership and shifting regulatory environments, the revolutionary role of user-generated content and digital convergence, and coverage of global issues by rolling news services.

Chapters include:

- a brief history of broadcasting;
- an overview of recent commercial challenges in the news industry and the impact on television news;
- current trends in the running of local radio stations, with particular focus on the rise of 'hubbing';
- the ethics of broadcast journalism;
- the significance of international broadcasters including the BBC, CNN and Al Jazeera.

The book identifies how the dissemination of broadcast journalism is evolving, whilst also arguing for the continued resilience of this industry now and in the future, making the case that journalistic storytelling remains at its most effective in broadcast environments. Professional journalists and students of media studies and journalism will find this a timely and thought-provoking intervention, which will help to inform their professional practice and research.

Stephen Jukes is Professor of Journalism at Bournemouth University, UK. His research focuses on objectivity and emotion in news with an emphasis on affect, trauma and conflict. A former foreign correspondent and Head of News at Reuters, he has edited a series of books on the Middle East and written extensively on journalism and trauma.

Katy McDonald is Director of Excellence in Learning and Teaching for the School of Arts and Cultures at Newcastle University, UK. A former broadcast journalist, her research interests include the effect on journalists of technological, financial and cultural changes in radio newsroom practices. She has published on newsroom 'hubbing' in UK commercial radio, and mediatisation.

Guy Starkey is Professor and Associate Dean Global Engagement at Bournemouth University, UK. His research interests include radio and journalism practices, institutions and technologies. A radio producer and presenter, his publications include *Radio Journalism* (2009, with Andrew Crisell) and *Radio in Context* (2013).

Understanding Broadcast Journalism

Stephen Jukes, Katy McDonald and Guy Starkey

Routledge
Taylor & Francis Group

LONDON AND NEW YORK

First published 2018
by Routledge
2 Park Square, Milton Park, Abingdon, Oxon OX14 4RN

and by Routledge
711 Third Avenue, New York, NY 10017

Routledge is an imprint of the Taylor & Francis Group, an informa business

British Library Cataloguing-in-Publication Data
A catalogue record for this book is available from the British Library

Library of Congress Cataloging-in-Publication Data
A catalog record for this title has been requested

ISBN: 9781138240995 (hbk)
ISBN: 9781138241008 (pbk)
ISBN: 9781315281650 (ebk)

Typeset in Sabon
by Out of House Publishing

MIX
Paper from responsible sources
FSC
www.fsc.org   FSC™ C013985

Printed in the United Kingdom
by Henry Ling Limited

Contents

Introduction

A scholarly work on the subject of broadcast journalism, especially one which is to be committed to paper, faces a number of challenges. The most obvious one is that of currency. Writing about a field which can change very rapidly, and publishing the work in a medium which is notorious for its lengthy production processes – the academic book – is almost to invite the subject matter to transform itself unrecognisably overnight. When writing the introduction to a previous book, *Local Radio, Going Global*, one of the authors noted the interesting coincidence of the word 'global' in the title also being the brand name of the UK's largest commercial radio group, Global Radio (Starkey, 2015: xi). It may be, he warned, that because change in the media industries can happen very fast, the group of radio stations might have rebranded itself with another name or been bought by another, even larger business entity, perhaps long before the print edition of the book was delivered by the printers. In fact, that didn't happen, and at the time of writing this new book, some seven years later, that same group remains the most significant on the UK commercial radio landscape. Despite a rather idiosyncratic decision to call its parent company This Is Global Limited, at the time of writing, the name 'Global' is even heard during every news bulletin broadcast by the radio stations it operates.

Such fortunate happenstance cannot, however, always be relied upon, and the question remains: how to ensure such a book as this remains current for long enough to justify the investment in it by the authors, the publisher and indeed the reader? In fact, the answer is simple. A name change is purely cosmetic, while the underlying principles of broadcast journalism have remained unchanged for decades. Even the introduction of new technology and the development of new platforms for the dissemination of journalistic *content* – a word to which we will return many times in this book – have done little to change the basic principles of storytelling through broadcasting. A second author worked for several years in a commercial radio newsroom, compiling and editing news bulletins in peak time, learning to cope with changing circumstances and consistently meeting the regular on-air deadlines that so obviously distinguish the broadcast variant from other forms of journalism. Even though since then the emphasis on putting content online and making it accessible on demand via mobile devices has grown considerably, as we shall argue, such modern methods of dissemination remain ancillary to the main activity of broadcasting in the broadcast journalism newsroom.

In terms of television, another advance in recent years has been the development of *internationalised* rolling news services such as RT, CGTN and Al Jazeera, which broadcast across national boundaries from Russia, China and Qatar respectively. Our third author worked around the world as a foreign correspondent and editor for the international news agency Reuters and gained a breadth of experience in presenting news stories using words and moving images in ways that would be instantly accessible to audiences in different national markets. These were often major breaking news stories with the potential to resonate globally in terms of both impact and influence. Yet these stories also called for explanation and contextualisation to make them understandable thousands of miles away from their epicentres. In short, each of the authors of this book has worked in and researched different areas of broadcast news journalism, focusing on our own specialisms, as the craft has continued to evolve since we began teaching it instead of practising it. This has, in turn, allowed us to develop an objectivity and a comprehensiveness in our approach to the subject that would not be possible if we were each still caught up in the minutiae of daily work routines in one medium or another. Of course, our research is not only academic but includes ongoing engagement in the profession, along with learning to use emerging software and innovative platforms, as well as networking with and interviewing current practitioners about their work.

Therefore, although the development of even newer software or changes in ownership of commercial radio, to cite but two examples, might threaten to damage the currency of a book which focuses exclusively upon such issues, the account which follows is more durable in many ways. This book identifies *trends* from which it is possible to extrapolate likely future developments and situates them in wider contexts, including the historical development of broadcast journalism and the complex relationship between journalism and society, rationalising along the way how current practice relates to the past, considering institutional, regulatory and societal influences on the profession and explaining how journalistic storytelling is best done in primarily *broadcast* environments.

Readers will find that the book is accessible in a number of ways, whether their interest is academic or professional – or both. It may, of course, be read in a linear fashion, from start to finish, much as one might consume a novel, although in this case the content is factual instead of fictional. Alternatively, and because broadcasting is not homogeneous – the same wherever it occurs – some readers may prefer to access only those chapters which relate to the sectors of broadcasting which most interest them, be they television, radio or online content, national or international approaches to storytelling, or even reasons why, as opposed to ways in which, broadcast journalism manifests itself as it does. Both the table of contents and the index have been prepared in order to best facilitate this.

Despite the often very practical nature of the content, *Understanding Broadcast Journalism* is not a manual or a course of instruction. Rather, it is an academic discussion of the nature of broadcast journalism, constructed in such a way as to promote *understanding* of its contexts and its characteristics, of its practices and its paradigms and of its methods and motivations. For those who practise broadcast journalism, or would do so in future, it should enable that practice to be informed by insight. For those who wish only to reflect on broadcast journalism, it should also provide a depth of understanding and underpinning knowledge necessary to enable sound analysis, argumentation and ultimately the drawing of appropriate conclusions.

Broadcast journalism, going digital

The most significant technological development in broadcast journalism in recent years has been the migration of its electronic production processes from the original analogue domain to digital. For those who have not experienced the previous, analogue, age, it might be difficult to comprehend the significance of such a change and to appreciate that the scale and pace of change were so great for those who lived through it that it now seems in retrospect little short of a revolution.

There are, of course, some, normally in the academic community rather than among practitioners, who would fondly suggest that what they might term 'technological determinism' is an inappropriate perspective from which to consider any electronic medium. They would argue that the technology is incidental to the practices which use it, that the equipment is merely a means to an end, and that of far greater importance in understanding it are the motivation and the psyche of each individual practitioner. That term, 'technological determinism', is frequently attributed to the economist and sociologist Thorstein Veblen (Riesman, 1953). Other technological determinists, depending on one's perspective, have included the communications theorist Marshall McLuhan (2001: 334), with his categorisation in the 1960s of 'hot' and 'cool' media, and his prediction that the world would shrink in communication terms to the size of a 'global village', in which electronic media enable individuals to feel they are close neighbours to others many thousands of miles away. It is unlikely that McLuhan could have imagined how right his predictions would, in essence, turn out to be, now that in the twenty-first century social networking platforms enable individuals to view with relative ease photographs of the cute cats and precocious children of complete strangers on the other side of the world. However, the theories of Veblen and McLuhan are frequently criticised as oversimplistic for their contention that much dramatic change in society can be attributed solely to the intervention of new technologies in media and communication.

Indeed, the critics of technological determinism do have a point. It is true that other influences on broadcast journalism worthy of note would include institutional, commercial and societal issues, such as over ownership of broadcasting organisations, their regulation by official bodies tasked and empowered with controlling them, or indeed prevailing attitudes in society over current controversies and ethics – the constantly shifting boundaries of what is considered to be acceptable behaviour by individuals and groups towards others. In dismissing the importance of technological advance, though, right is probably not on their side, because, as *Understanding Broadcast Journalism* contends, all such factors are in their own ways significant. Although technology is not the only determining factor in the development of broadcast journalism, it is nonetheless of considerable significance. Furthermore, it can be argued that change in society often results from a range of influences, but in turn it may sometimes be journalism that most impacts on society, rather than *vice versa*. Chapter 4 considers to what extent the existence of new practices and new platforms might really have changed broadcast journalism from its emergent forms of the early twentieth century, or whether it is still, at its core, unchanged.

To return to the technology of broadcast journalism, to believe that change to the means of production and distribution will have an impact on what is produced and disseminated requires no great leap of faith. In fact, it has been observable – particularly over the past twenty years – and recordable. In picture archives and published work, still images proliferate of the large, bulky and normally quite immovable production equipment of the birth of mass-market 'wireless' broadcasting in the 1920s (Street, 2002). When the second electronic medium of mass communication, radio, was born, production was largely studio-bound, simply because of the difficulty inherent in moving that equipment away from its permanent base. Microphones were exclusively positioned on a desktop, rather than hand-held. They were built with a sensitivity to extraneous noise, either ambient or accidental, that discouraged producers and presenters alike from moving them except when turned off. The other apparatus found in the radio studio was similarly difficult to move because of its size, as was the domestic radio receiver, which in the 1920s was typically as large as a 1980s box-shaped television set and either connected to electrical mains power or further weighed down by cumbersome battery packs that could not be replaced other than by returning them to the shop for recharging behind the sales counter. Soon, mains-powered sets took over from battery-powered units, so for the next thirty years the 'wireless' was most definitely connected to the wall by an electrical lead. In fact, the only way this technology could really be described as 'wireless' was in the way the broadcast signal was distributed over what seemed then like incredibly large distances via a transmitter, and then through the air to an aerial either inside or on top of the home.

The development of the smaller, more compact and more easily transportable transistor radio in the 1960s was a technological change that relocated radio listening out of the living room, where it had been a communal activity, to the bedroom, the bathroom, the kitchen and even the car. This was rather fortunate for the medium of radio because another new invention, the television set, had already begun to displace the radio receiver from pride of place in the living room and its well-established status of focal point for the family's evening entertainment (Starkey, 2014: 384–385). Television technology had also developed consistently over time, so the original wobbly 405-line black-and-white pictures projected onto the screen at the front of another large box were eventually replaced by higher-definition 625-line transmissions in colour using an increasingly flatter, more truly rectangular, cathode ray tube screen to show its pictures to growing audiences.

Those pictures were made up of 625 horizontal lines, most of which could be seen by the viewer if sitting too close to it, and they represented a step change in picture definition from the previous, 405-line, system. Today's flatscreen technology, using LCD or LED illumination of the perfectly rectangular image, and even curved 4K Ultra HD screens, seems light years away from the now all-but-extinct cathode ray tube, and represents a further step change in media technology – as in turn did the arrival of satellite, cable and IPTV.[1] Once television cameras became portable and thus usable on location, celluloid film, which required developing in a lab before it could be shown as part of a television programme, began to be replaced in the 1970s by 'electronic newsgathering'. This meant on-location television reporting could now be more easily done live, and the greater immediacy of television news which resulted from the development allowed reporters and editors to set new standards in newsgathering and storytelling.

Every one of those technological advances – and more – seemed at the time to be groundbreaking, just like the introduction of FM radio transmissions in stereo, the development of on-screen teletext, and the discovery in the 1980s that a remote control makes changing television channels much easier than getting up each time to push a button or turn a dial on the TV set itself. However, it was the quickening pace of change to broadcast media technology that began in the late 1980s with the introduction of 'personal' computers into the studio and the newsroom that made the move from analogue to digital so significant, as well, of course, as the myriad new opportunities it brought to the specific activity of broadcast journalism. Chapters 2 and 3 consider in greater detail issues around technology and how it is used by broadcast journalists, but it is important to note in passing that the broadcast media were not alone in benefiting from technological change. Print, including not only newspapers and magazines but also, in time, books, pamphlets and even posters, experienced dramatic change in production and distribution processes with the move in the 1980s from (literally) hot-metal typesetting to photographic and then completely electronic page layout. This enabled not only the development of colour photography in newspapers (most controversially in the UK with the launch of the national daily *Today* by the regional newspaper owner Eddy Shah) but also in-country printing of, for example, different editions of such global titles as the *International Herald Tribune*.[2]

The personal computer, and later, of course, the laptop, the tablet and even the smartphone, enabled reporters to write copy on location or at home and then submit it over the Internet to a newsroom. Subsequently, they could even post copy and images directly online, without them being seen first by a sub-editor – often with consequences of only linguistic, but sometimes also of legal, significance. Of course, readers too began to acquire these new forms of digital communication technology and to change the way they accessed the various output of print journalism. Some 'newspaper' content is now distinctly 'multimedia' in nature, as genres and subgenres from the broadcast media are adopted by 'print' journalists in order to enhance their online presence. The launch of *Today* in 1986 was controversial, not only because the colour images that drew widespread attention to its launch were initially rather fuzzy and the colour in its photographs somewhat less than realistic, but also because the introduction of its then modern print processes involved a protracted industrial relations dispute with trade unionists, who perceived in them, not incorrectly, a more widespread threat to existing working practices elsewhere in the industry.

Several national newspaper titles had already been the focus of industrial unrest when in January of that same year the largest newspaper group in the UK, News International, had moved its print operation to a new, fortified production centre in the east of London, dubbed by many 'Fortress Wapping'. Because newspapers, like the first electronic medium of mass communication, film, were wholly dependent for distribution on transportation by rail and road, a new fleet of lorries was commissioned to transport them under police escort out of Wapping (Starkey, 2007: 47). Unfortunately for News International owner Rupert Murdoch and others, the benefits of the new print technology of the 1980s have probably been outweighed by the inexorable rise in consumer access to electronic digital communication technology because far fewer people are now prepared to *buy* a newspaper than in the preceding decades and collecting payment for content accessed online is notoriously difficult. Chapter 1 considers some of the disadvantages for the print media of emerging media technologies, most notably falling newspaper circulation and, consequently, loss of income and the effect that has had on the ambitions and the quality of its journalism.

Political economy

If technology is not the whole story, though, what else does it include? Understanding most kinds of journalism requires an appreciation of the fact that somebody has to pay for it to take place. There are exceptions, of course, because, as in many sectors of economic activity, there are situations in which some people are prepared to work without payment. That is as true in the high-street retail sector (where normally charity shops are staffed by volunteers) as it is in the media, where community radio stations, for example, typically are run mostly by unpaid enthusiasts. Online, there are lone individuals who post self-generated content because of some passion they have for their subject that in their minds renders actual payment for their efforts unnecessary – as well as in most cases probably unlikely. Cost, however, is not normally confined to human resources, although paying for staff or freelancers to work as journalists, presenters, administrators, technicians and so on is usually the most expensive burden on a broadcasting organisation's finances.

Even the humblest of community radio stations requires money, in the form of capital to resource its start-up, and in the form of revenue from whatever source to pay for ongoing and incidental expenses incurred in running the business. These include the studio, the equipment, the licence to broadcast and the sum paid to acquire from the regulator the licence to broadcast, as well as heating, lighting, transmission and so on – even if volunteers clean the premises themselves to save money, as well as being responsible for making content. Similarly, the lone web content creator is using resources that cost somebody money – namely the computer, its connectivity with the Internet via a service provider, and the inevitable electricity, heating and lighting required to make the premises tolerable, however humble they may be.

Such economic realities are not unconnected with the need felt by Eddy Shah to sell *Today* to a company called Lonrho a few months after its launch, and in turn for Lonrho to sell it to Rupert Murdoch in 1987, who finally closed it in 1995. The newspaper was more a victim of a crowded national daily newspaper market then than of newer media. It was a market which also saw launches of the ill-fated *Sunday Correspondent* and *News on Sunday*, both titles folding within months of their launch; of the *European*, which probably failed to embrace the *zeitgeist* of the 1990s; and of the *Sunday Sport* and *Daily Sport* – for whose rather more salacious content of semi-pornography and so-called 'false' news there proved to be more of an appetite, because they are still being published today (Starkey, 2007: 48). In Chapter 1, industry circulation data will be used to demonstrate how in the ten years between 2006 and 2016 actual falls in established newspaper circulation due to changes in consumer habits have, in the case of some UK national dailies, been as drastic as 50%.

That some newspapers should have closed in the past, or be perilously close to closure today, is not particularly remarkable when different sectors of the media industries are compared with others. While the growth of Internet use and the number of competing sources even of mainstream journalistic content has been notable over the period identified as the 'digital revolution', so too has the rise of the online advertising market and the number of advertisers who have transferred some or all of their advertising budget out of traditional media and into this new environment. Similarly, this has impacted upon not only the share of audience of radio and television broadcasters, but also the advertising revenues of those who depend upon such incomes for their survival. As the number of radio stations and television channels has increased at a far greater rate than the number of newspaper titles ever could, because of the more challenging economics of printing and distributing printed products by road, there have been spectacular failures, as cherished radio and television brands have disappeared in response to the often harsh effects of market competition.

In the United Kingdom, even the BBC, which does not depend on domestic advertising for its income because of its public sector status and its particular funding method – the television licence fee – has been subject to a squeeze on its income. This has resulted in the cutting of several budgets and part-closure of its broadcast channel BBC Three.[3] Cost-cutting efficiencies have also trimmed the budgets of local radio, as programme-sharing across wider regions and subregions has ended some local programme production and, hence, some of the uniqueness of most of those radio stations. Distinctive to the United Kingdom, though, this has not been as a result of increased competition from other organisations or newer platforms but of governmental decision-making, behind which lies a Conservative Party that is ideologically opposed to an expanding public sector and is a vigorous supporter of private enterprise. By cutting the real-terms value of the licence fee, and allocating to the BBC's budget costs which were previously borne by governments – such as the BBC World Service and free television licences for over-75s – the BBC has suffered from actions which are at least partly politically motivated as opposed to being attributable to economic and societal factors alone.

Such effects as falling circulations, decreasing advertising revenue and the closure of newspapers, radio stations and television channels do not impact solely upon their owners, staff and audiences. They are implicated in the wider phenomenon of the so-called 'political economy', in which economics and politics are both intertwined and interdependent. Because Rupert Murdoch, for example, still controls the largest share of the national daily newspaper audience in the United Kingdom, he still has potentially the greatest opportunity to influence the views of more newspaper readers than anyone else. That is an opportunity that both he and his editors often exploit in order to influence the course of political events in what is otherwise a democracy. Chapter 1 further discusses how the relatively unregulated newspaper industry contrasts with the highly regulated environment of broadcasting – a quite common feature of many Western democracies – and how this impacts on the importance of journalism that is broadcast.

At this point it will suffice to bear in mind that, although Murdoch owned a sizeable stake in the satellite and cable operator BSkyB since its creation by merger, UK legislation requires Sky – as it is known more widely – to be subject to regulation by the Office of Communications (Ofcom). This is true of all the UK-licensed broadcasters, even though Sky's satellite TV signal is broadcast *to* the UK from *outside* its jurisdiction. In reality, the geostationary satellites that Sky uses for its direct-to-home broadcasts are positioned in a region of space that is allocated to Luxembourg for that purpose, echoing the days of Radio Luxembourg and other continental 'pirate' radio stations that once broke the BBC's monopoly of radio broadcasting by transmitting to the UK from countries elsewhere in Europe (Crisell, 1994: 17–41). In 2017, the UK government had to decide whether to allow Murdoch to buy the rest of Sky through his 21st Century Fox group or whether his owner-ship of that company as well as the renamed News UK newspaper group would be too great a concentration of media power and consequently a threat to media pluralism. There is a broad consensus in Western democra-cies that pluralism – or a multiplicity of voices through diversity of owner-ship – is desirable in ensuring no one organisation or individual accumulates an unfair level of influence over the 'public sphere' identified by the German sociologist and philosopher Jürgen Habermas (1989).

Many of the philosophical theories of political economy that remain pop-ular today can be traced back to the writings of Karl Marx, who placed a particular emphasis on the idea that economic control brought clear advan-tages in the communication of messages (Murdock & Golding, 1977: 15). His focus was on the ownership of factories as being influential on large numbers of working-class people; but it is hard to look at the ownership of newspapers today, as well as in the years since Marx wrote about political economy, and the way newspapers tend to promote certain causes and polit-ical parties over others, and not be tempted to argue that Marx had a point with that core idea of ownership being related to potential influence. Like McLuhan in the 1960s, Marx could not have imagined the scale and the diversity of the media industries of today.

Which journalism, where?

Despite the apparent diminution of the power of the press in recent years due to falling circulations and the proliferation of alternative media, the news-paper industry has fought back. The most tangible sign of this has been the emergence of the 'freesheets' which are given away without any attempt to collect revenue through a cover price, and even the conversion of some pre-viously paid-for titles into freesheets, most notably in the United Kingdom in the case of the London *Evening Standard*. Newspaper content, most of it free, is widely available online. Undoubtedly, though, the main challenger to newspaper journalism, and to a lesser extent broadcast journalism, has come from exclusively online sources. Effectively, now 'newspaper' owner-ship is no longer the preserve of those with very deep pockets – if, that is, it is only online. These new competitors include a vast array of news websites, some of them producing original content such as the *Huffington Post*, and others which are merely news-aggregators which, either manually or using an algorithm to do it automatically, simply collect and re-present content from other sites, be they operated by newspapers, broadcasters or any other type of organisation or individual. The print industry is more challenged than ever before, and quite possibly just as interesting.

The focus of this book is, however, on *broadcast* journalism. That is, to give it a definition, those many forms of contemporary journalism which originate from organisations whose primary concern is broadcasting, and whose secondary concern may be repurposing their primary content in order to enhance their online presence. This will, of course, be examined in detail in later chapters, and most extensively in Chapter 4, but, as will become apparent, there are sufficient peculiarities to *broadcast* journalism to justify a book such as this being dedicated to it, rather than any kind of discussion of this variant of the practice being confined to more general analyses of journalism in which it risks being marginalised – or even from which it might be excluded altogether. The point of *convergence* (another term which recurs in subsequent chapters) between broadcast and print journalism of many kinds and genres is now that online manifestation of it, which is arguably as important to broadcasters as it is to 'print' journalists.

Despite the way in which it is often discussed, such convergence is not an exclusively recent phenomenon, and predates even the invention of the Internet. In the now seemingly distant past, broadcasting organisations had – sometimes tentatively, sometimes confidently – involved themselves in publishing. And publishers have experimented with broadcasting. For example, in the United Kingdom a radio station now owned by the country's second-largest group of commercial radio stations, Bauer Media (at the time branded as Red Rose Radio in Preston), launched an advertising-driven local newspaper entitled the *Preston Red Rose Advertiser*, which lasted for three years from 1987–1990. Another station, 106.7 Kestrel FM, launched a more news-orientated weekly from an early 'bi-media' newsroom, the *Basingstoke Observer* in 1998. Conversely, in 2001 the *Kent Messenger* local newspaper began acquiring, then operating and finally consolidating through programme-sharing, a total of seven commercial radio stations in South East England, every one of them now branded with the acronym kmfm (Starkey & Crisell, 2009: 78). These examples were, though, in the context of the United Kingdom, limited exceptions to the rule, and it was only through the arrival and subsequent popular exploitation of the Internet that convergence of broadcast and print journalism began in earnest.

So, for many sound reasons, including its significance, its potential to survive and the career opportunities it offers – rather than simply a personal predilection on the authors' part – the book will focus on broadcast journalism and also refer where appropriate to other forms of journalism, much as has been the case in this brief introduction. In writing it, another pertinent question has been one of geographical coverage. As all three authors have worked in journalism in the United Kingdom and have conducted extensive research on the country's media industries, it seems natural that most of the cases cited will be from the United Kingdom. That is one way to ensure consistency across the whole book, and to provide a more coherent and lucid account of how broadcast journalism has developed and how it manifests itself in an interrelated and increasingly convergent media landscape. This approach is, though, intended to be both accessible and useful to readers in other territories, and so two additional strategies have been adopted: referring to international issues and global perspectives wherever they are relevant in this increasingly *geographically* convergent world, and providing a limited number of examples from other countries wherever to do so would be prudent in the way that it might better illuminate some particular point or demonstrate that a particular phenomenon has the potential to be generalised to wider contexts.

Drawing conclusions

Inevitably, the discussion above, which attempts to set the scene for the rest of the book, is necessarily superficial in its analysis. The main themes will be revisited later, as appropriate. Furthermore, neither technological advance nor political economy as so far discussed exist in a vacuum nor indeed do they enjoy an exclusive role in the development of broadcast journalism. To further extend and develop this analysis, Chapter 5 considers the range of practices discussed throughout the book within a much wider range of contexts; Chapter 6 explores a number of ethical issues to which practitioner and academic audiences alike should pay attention. Pertinent to both is the relatively new issue of user-generated content, or UGC. The technological advances discussed earlier in this introduction have not just revolutionised working practices for professional journalists, but they have also provided opportunities for others to indulge in journalism – or at least to contribute to it. Just as people without any professional training as journalists may now create their own web content and post it online for others to discover, they may even through happenstance witness and manage to capture potentially useful content and offer it to established journalists to use. This can often be more graphic or compelling than a journalist arriving at the scene much later could acquire by traditional means, making it especially attractive to editors, despite potential pitfalls in relying on it as a substantial source.

One early example of UGC playing a significant role in reporting breaking news occurred when coordinated terrorist attacks on 7 July 2005 led to the detonation of improvised bombs on the London Underground. On BBC Radio 5 Live, presenter Nicky Campbell was hosting the regular early-morning phone-in when reports from the public began to reach the studio. As the radio station's broadcast format allows the interruption of scheduled programming and planned items when breaking news warrants it, Campbell was given short announcements to read out, explaining that some sort of incident had occurred at an Underground station. The initially sketchy information being phoned in to the BBC by listeners began to be supplemented by tentative initial statements from the emergency services and the local government authority, Transport for London, as reporters for the BBC and other news organisations started to contact them for clarification of the situation. Within twenty minutes of the first report, the previous phone-in topic was abandoned and the programme became rolling news coverage of the carnage that was taking place on and underneath the streets of London. Eyewitness accounts of news events have long contributed to journalistic practice, since even the birth of the newspaper, but the immediacy of the mobile phone and the growing willingness of members of the public to spontaneously offer content to journalists in all media have greatly increased the potential of such sources. There has been a parallel increase in their ability to capture and send still images, audio and video, all of which may be used by trained journalists in their print, broadcast and online reporting.

The ethical issues which arise from such developing practices in journalism are, though, quite considerable. They include the decisions a journalist must take over whether to use them, their authenticity, any issues over representation, impartiality, intellectual property rights, possible invasion of privacy and even the technical quality of such content, because professionalism normally requires standards of lighting, framing, sound capture, aspect ratio, focus and even the absence of camera shake that are unlikely to be at the forefront of the mind of the amateur reporter during a moment of high drama. This so-called 'citizen journalism' has at times been portrayed as fortuitous, opportunistic and authentic because it has the instant appearance of a genuine eyewitness account. At other times it has been seen as naïve, under-researched, lacking the fact-checking and triangulation of information that experienced reporters should normally apply to their journalism – and occasionally deliberately misleading. The new trend at the time of writing this book for even popular websites of some repute to publish 'fake news' should reinforce concerns about truthfulness, and there is now ever greater potential for rumour and pure fiction to confuse and contradict professional journalists and the public alike. Before using what appears to be good, engaging user-generated content, a number of decisions have to be taken over whether using it is the correct and proper response to receiving it in the newsroom.

Such dilemmas have existed over more recent events, such as the murder by extremists of the army drummer, Fusilier Lee Rigby, on a London street in 2013, the aftermath of which was captured on video by members of the public who witnessed the killing – especially as that video content gave the killers a platform to make political statements to camera, attempting to justify their actions as they stood over the body. It is arguable to what extent that UGC simply did the work of the extremists by publicising their cause and the ideology behind their actions, with the possibility of inciting further such publicity-seeking or copycat activity. Of course, there exists a counterargument that any kind of publicity generated for extremists by journalistic activity, whether user-generated or not, can be potentially harmful to wider society. Nevertheless, it is legitimate to question what purpose is served by including citizen contributions in the coverage of war – such as mobile phone footage of dead bodies resulting from the aerial bombing by Syria and Russia of the eastern rebel-held area of Aleppo in 2016, or the use by Syria of chemical weapons against the population of Ghouta in 2013. Such fundamental debates around notions of 'right' and 'wrong' lie at the heart of ethical debates in journalism generally and quite specifically in broadcast journalism, not least given its instantaneous nature and the need to make snap editorial decisions.

The conclusion of *Understanding Broadcast Journalism* attempts to pull together many of these issues in a logical and systematic way which sums up the main ideas in the book and draws some appropriate and robust reasoning from them which is practical, generalisable and durable. It asks whether broadcast journalism faces a future that can truly be considered to be broadcast, or whether it is destined for one which is increasingly multiplatformed, nuanced and time-shifted – while remaining sufficiently authoritative to be consistent with its often-Reithian origins. Firstly, though, and despite the incontrovertible ability of the reader to subvert this plan, the next chapter addresses in greater detail some of the fundamentals of broadcast journalism, beginning with the importance of the role it can play in democratic societies.

Notes

1 Internet Protocol TV refers to the ability to deliver television content over the Internet, as opposed to terrestrial, satellite or cable formats.
2 The newspaper was known as the *International Herald Tribune* from 1967 to 2013, when it was renamed as the *International New York Times*. It has subsequently been renamed again to reflect its underlying ownership as the *New York Times International Edition*.
3 It ceased operations on 16 February 2016 and was replaced by an online-only version.

Chapter bibliography

Crisell, A. (1994) *Understanding Radio*. London: Routledge.
Habermas, J. (1989) *The Structural Transformation of the Public Sphere*. Cambridge: Polity.
McLuhan, M. (2001) *Understanding Media: The Extensions of Man*. London: Routledge (first published 1964).
Murdock, G. and Golding, P. (1977) 'Capitalism, Communication and Class Relations' *in:* Curran, J. et al. (eds) *Mass Communication and Society*, pp. 12–43. London: Arnold.
Riesman, D. (1953) *Thorstein Veblen: A Critical Interpretation*, New York: Scribner.

Starkey, G. (2007) *Balance and Bias in Journalism: Regulation, Representation and Democracy*. London: Palgrave Macmillan.

Starkey, G. (2014) 'Radio's audiences' *in:* Conboy, M. and Steel, J. (eds) *The Routledge Companion to British Media History*. London: Routledge.

Starkey, G. (2015) *Local Radio, Going Global*. London: Palgrave Macmillan.

Starkey, G. and Crisell, A. (2009) *Radio Journalism*. London: Sage.

Street, S. (2002) *A Concise History of British Radio*. Tiverton: Kelly Publications.

1　The importance of being broadcast

The nature of broadcasting

As this book is about *broadcast* journalism, it is appropriate to begin by
considering what is meant by the adjective 'broadcast', the verb 'to broadcast' and the noun 'broadcasting'. The number of different ways of accessing
media content has proliferated over recent years, so it would not be surprising if younger generations began to emerge with little real understanding of the meaning of broadcasting. Put simply, and in its broadest sense,
broadcasting is the dissemination of media content over a wide enough area
to cover neighbourhoods, communities, towns, regions, whole countries or
continents without any need for a physical connection between the origi-
nator and the recipient. That is why the developing medium of radio was
originally, in the 1920s, called the 'wireless' (Crisell, 1994). Broadcasting
usually refers to sound or a combination of sound and vision, but encoded
data have been included in broadcast transmissions since the addition of
teletext in the 1970s to television screens in order to provide scrolling pages
of information – some of it journalistic in nature – and, because of its apparent immediacy, at the time this was quite an innovation.

Similarly, in the 1980s the Radio Data System (RDS) began to add
basic display information, such as the name of the station, and to divert
car radios to retune from the programme being listened to, to another, to
provide local traffic and travel information at different times of the day.
Nonetheless, broadcasting is (and always has been) in most cases something
that is offered to anybody within its coverage area to be tuned in to free of
charge, and the broadcast signal is unaffected by the number of receivers in
that area that are tuned into it. There could be just a single person listening
to or watching a given transmission at any time, or a million, and the size of
the audience would make no difference to the quality or availability of the
transmission – whereas a live stream or any kind of data transfer using the
Internet is limited in terms of the number of devices that can connect to it
at any one time.

This distinction between the use of electromagnetic waves distributed
through the atmosphere to transmit content and the relatively simple

sending and receiving of data transmissions back and forth along either copper wires or fibre-optic cable is an important one. For some, who might be called purists, broadcasting will always have only its original meaning, dating back to the days when in the late 1890s Marconi first demonstrated the ability to send rudimentary but essentially meaningful 'content' in the form of Morse code over long distances (Street, 2002). The content may have changed dramatically, becoming much more sophisticated and soon used to communicate with many people at a time, rather than a means of one-to-one messaging as Marconi had originally envisaged it. But listening to the radio requires a box with an aerial on top in order to be radio. In the same way, intrinsic to watching television is a larger box connected to an outside aerial, carefully directed at a distant point from which the transmissions originate. Others will take a more liberal view of the term, noting that the radio began to appear in large numbers of cars in the 1960s, as the technology that underpinned the 'platform' shrank dramatically in size with the development of the transistor – a tiny electrical component that replaced the huge, glowing valves inside the very first wirelesses of the first half of the twentieth century (Starkey, 2014). The television aerial, too, began to be supplemented from the late 1980s on many dwellings by a satellite dish and, at about the same time, both television and radio programmes became 'time-shiftable' through the use of cassette tapes that could capture the broadcasts and enable them to be enjoyed later, or played back repeatedly, or even fast-forwarded and rewound according to the predilection of the listener or viewer.

Suddenly, media that were previously only consumed in a linear, once-only, catch-it-now-or-miss-it fashion, were becoming non-linear. But their audiences did not consider they were now consuming something new. To them these were still radio and television. Soon it was common for mobile phones to include within their circuitry an FM radio receiver, so small had the technology become. Doubling up as an aerial is the earphone cable, with this modern, miniature radio set also sharing the phone's touch-screen user interface. Even though the marketing for the device describes it as a phone, and its primary use is normally as a phone, it is in essence just as much a radio as any other box with an aerial on top that can receive and play out FM transmissions. Today's modern smartphone is capable of receiving live radio and television as streamed data, as opposed to an analogue radio wave, and playing it out using the loudspeaker and, in the case of television, the screen. To complicate the issue for purists, the digitally-encoded data that carries the radio, television and also any phone calls arrive at the phone's built-in aerial on an analogue radio wave – one which is dissimilar to an FM transmission only in length and height. In fact, all of the data received and sent by the phone rely on analogue radio waves to make the journey to and from the nearest mobile phone mast, but they are waves which carry digitally-encoded information. If the receiving equipment is a laptop or a desktop computer or a digital television set connected by a wire to a data network, it is further evidence of the blurring of boundaries between what would once have been considered to be discrete, or completely separate, technologies.

That blurring of boundaries over the past twenty years or so is commonly referred to as 'convergence', and it is difficult to predict what further convergence will occur in even the very near future, so rapid has been the pace of change. Whether we will still commonly refer to certain forms of media content as 'television' or 'radio' in a few years' time is uncertain, but in fact they are useful labels for describing the way content is framed, arranged and presented. To be pedantic for a moment, when people say they are watching television, they are usually referring to the content *on* the television set, rather than watching the television *set* itself. Listening intently to a radio *set* that is turned off would not be a particularly rewarding experience, so when they say they are listening to radio, they really mean they are listening to the various sound elements that have been assembled into a particular order, mixed, faded up and faded down in ways that are recognised as displaying the common codes and conventions of radio broadcasting. Radio programming can sound more or less the same, whether or not it is coming from a small box with an aerial or a laptop, just as television programming may not change through being viewed and heard through a tablet or iPad. Some media producers go further than this common multiplatform approach to distributing their content, and exploit their brands through different but complementary content for different platforms. In the United Kingdom, the BBC creates visual live and on-demand content under its youth-focused Radio 1 brand, as does Global – a company which has dropped the word 'radio' from its different radio brands, identified only as Heart, Smooth and Capital, even though it is content that uses mainly established radio codes and conventions to communicate with its audiences and the company shows music videos on parallel satellite and cable television channels operating under the same brands.

Such big operators as the BBC and Global are not the only broadcasters to routinely disseminate parallel time-shiftable and extended content online through other, essentially mobile, platforms that are complementary to the broadcast output of their television and radio platforms. For a radio station to own a complementary television channel, even to run relatively cheap music video programming continuously, requires deep pockets. However, most radio and television services run much cheaper website operations in order to extend the brand to another platform, to make certain content – especially their journalism – instantly available, and to act as a conduit for interactivity between the audience and the broadcaster. Typical content for a website might include: instant access to the most recent news bulletin broadcast; a live stream enabling viewing or listening without access to a radio or a television set; an archive of past programmes, perhaps searchable by date or key words; extended content, such as the full-length version of an interview that was edited for broadcast due to lack of airtime; and a blog or podcast featuring highlights of past programmes or a background profile of a news story or an individual. It would be wrong to assume that such relatively sophisticated parallel content is only made available in the most developed of countries since, for example, in parts of Africa the radio station and its website may be the only source of locally-produced media content (Damome, 2011).

The term 'broadcasting' contrasts markedly, of course, with 'narrowcasting', one that was unkindly applied to some very early cable television experiments in the 1970s because their potential audiences were tiny compared to those of the few mainstream television channels on air then. 'Narrowcasting' could equally be applied now to some specialist or 'niche' programme-makers who reach very few people at a time because they are among the less popular options in a now very crowded media landscape. In short, the always-on availability of radio and television transmissions using electromagnetic waves that travel through the air to communicate their content, rather than wires or fibre-optic connections, has unlimited potential to build audiences – unlike the one-to-one nature of Internet, wifi and mobile phone connections, which means they have only a finite capacity to transmit and receive data to and from individual devices. When that capacity is exceeded, online streaming services simply cannot accept any further data traffic, and so reject any additional requests to connect to them. This greater potential of broadcasting to connect with unlimited audiences has particularly important implications for journalism at times of crisis or national disaster, as will be explained later.

Why *broadcast* journalism?

What, then, are the implications for journalism of *being* broadcast? And why is the act of broadcasting any form of journalism inherently significant? To answer these questions requires a thorough examination of broadcast journalism and of the environment in which it takes place – including the ways in which it relates to the other forms of journalism with which it competes for attention. Like all journalism, the importance of the broadcast variety derives in part from the need in democratic societies for citizens to have sufficient access to *information* and informed *comment* to participate fully in society, but also to be able to distinguish between the two. Information consists of one or more hard facts that enjoy some level of incontrovertibility, depending on the subject matter and the robustness of any proof underlying them, while informed comment is opinion provided by someone whose perspective may be treated with some confidence because they ought to know what they are talking about.

Depending on the credentials and the credibility of someone commenting on a situation, their opinions can carry more or less weight. US president Donald Trump, for example, has been very critical of most of the mainstream media in the United States and made it clear that he viewed their coverage of his presidency as biased. At the same time, his view was not universally shared in what the 2016 election showed to be a divided nation. And, sometimes, distinguishing between information and comment is genuinely difficult, especially when audiences are unable to use their primary senses to see, hear, smell or feel for themselves what has happened – as they might if they were at the scene of a major incident. It is here that an essential characteristic of journalism comes into the argument: the notion that the journalist acts as a proxy for the audience, relaying a more or less faithful version of the reality the journalist perceives, to the audience, on the audience's behalf (Starkey, 2007: xvii). That proxy – or representative – is clearly able at times to deliberately or unknowingly distort the truth, but 'ethical' or 'responsible' journalists would try not to do that, even by accident.

This book argues that in a world in which the various 'truths' underlying journalism are increasingly being challenged, broadcasting environments often offer the greatest chance of journalism being 'truthful', and therefore can be of greatest service to democracies and their peoples. That is one particularly good reason to contend that broadcast journalism is a positive influence on the world in which we live. But this sense of optimism can no longer be maintained lightly – both television and radio face serious challenges if they are to live up to this role in the future. Despite broadcasting's resilience as a dominant medium, discussed in detail below (see pp. 23–30), there are worrying concerns that young people are deserting traditional broadcast news. At the same time, competitive pressures are impinging on all sectors of broadcast news, whether this be delivered by commercial providers or those operating in a sheltered, and often highly regulated, public-service broadcasting environment. Such regulation can sometimes go a long way to supporting the democratic role of broadcasting, usually applying a set of commonly agreed rules and standards to all broadcasters in the country or region, and ensuring that they adhere largely to the rules and uphold the standards that are expected of them. In the United Kingdom, for example, this role is performed by the Office of Communications (Ofcom), which was set up by an Act of Parliament in 2003 and was preceded by the complementary bodies, the Radio Authority and the Independent Television Commission (1991–2003) and before them the Independent Broadcasting Authority (1972–1990) and the Independent Television Authority (1954–1972). The very names of these august bodies suggest the importance with which they were regarded in government, and they have each had the power at some stage to appoint or reject commercial radio and television broadcasters by giving or denying them licences to broadcast their programmes.

Licences could – and still can – be taken away in the event of the very worst breaches of the rules, and fines can be imposed for lesser offences, for example the broadcasting of swear words at inappropriate times of the day. Needless to say, major transgressions on the part of the operating companies have been very few and far between since commercial television began in the United Kingdom in 1955, because to lose a licence to broadcast would bring with it damaging consequences for the company that owns it. However, there have been very few serious suggestions that regulating broadcasting in this way has resulted in any systematic compromising of the standards of journalism in the commercial sector. Until the 2017 renewal of the BBC's Royal Charter, under which it is granted permission every ten years to broadcast radio and television to the UK, the BBC was largely responsible for regulating itself, but the principle of needing to adhere to a set of rules and standards has nonetheless applied to the Corporation since it was first granted a charter in 1927.

This dual-track approach to broadcasting in the United Kingdom, with a public sector loosely controlled and owned at 'arm's length' by the state, and a competing private sector owned by commercial interests, can be found in many parts of the world – notably in the countries of Western Europe, where private television and radio became increasingly popular during the 1970s. In France, for example, some of the biggest television audiences watch the state-owned France Télévision's offering of France 2, France 3, France 5 and France Ô, while Radio France operates several national radio stations, including France Inter, France Culture and France Musique. Parallel to those choices are many commercial television and radio companies broadcasting in competition with them, such as the hugely popular TF1, as well as Canal Plus, M6 and BFM on television, and RTL, Radio Monte-Carlo and Radio Fil Bleu. Just as in the United Kingdom, there is also a small, but interesting, community radio sector, run largely by volunteers on a not-for-profit basis. Many informed commentators, such as Crisell (2004), would contend that maintaining rival sectors in broadcasting drives up standards, as the commercial sector tries to match those of the public broadcasters and the public broadcasters try to attract similarly large audiences as the commercial sector's with equally popular programmes.

The BBC is funded by a television-receiving licence fee, payable by each household and business which operates at least one television set or live streaming television service. This guaranteed funding means it is not dependent on audience size to attract advertising income to pay for its operations. But as subsequent chapters discuss, even public-sector broadcasters are not immune from commercial pressures. And if audiences fell dramatically, politicians and rival media would be the first to question the justification for the licence fee. By contrast, Channel 4 – with its various associated channels such as E4, More4, Film4 and 4Music – is state-owned but funded by advertising. Since its launch in 1982 it has had a brief to provide distinctive, original and challenging programming, a central feature of its schedules being *Channel 4 News*, broadcast nightly in peak time at 7pm and running for just under an hour. Its extended duration allows a depth and breadth of coverage unattainable elsewhere, without the repetition of 'rolling news', which is considered in more detail later. Although the production company behind the programme, ITN, also produces shorter and arguably less challenging early-evening news programmes for rival channels ITV and Channel 5, its ability to do different kinds of broadcast journalism for different contexts and audiences of the three competing channels is both admirable and a demonstration of the versatility of the genre.

Only very rarely does Ofcom step in, in response to a complaint about something which has been broadcast. Indeed, the history of regulation in the UK has seen governments progressively loosening the grip of regulation over time, largely in response to demands from the private sector for more freedom to exercise their own judgment. Regulation is now mainly *reactive* to complaints or surveys investigating levels of satisfaction and media usage, but this wasn't always the case. The first regulators of what was initially called Independent Television, the ITA and the IBA, would vet programmes that were likely to be controversial *before* they were broadcast, demanding cuts and even banning programmes from being aired in exceptional circumstances. One such example was the 1971 *World in Action* documentary, *South of the Border* (Granada), which included interviews with known terrorists and, following a campaign in the press, was banned without even being viewed first (BFI, 2001). The IBA was, in effect, an expanded ITA, as it was newly tasked with introducing commercial radio to the United Kingdom from 1973. It required the new advertising-funded stations to seek permission even for any changes to programme schedules or the durations and timing of news bulletins *before* they were implemented – a firm grip on content that would be inconceivable to the station managers of today. The reason for this initially tight regulation of broadcasting came from a sense of responsibility towards stakeholders. The frequencies that could be used to broadcast, it was maintained, were scarce, and therefore the privilege to be able to broadcast on them brought with it a responsibility to use them in ways that would be fair to all. That didn't just mean maintaining agreed standards of taste and decency in programming, but it also meant being impartial between different shades of political opinion and over matters of public controversy (Starkey, 2007: 42–45).

That scarcity-of-frequencies argument was for many decades one which held true. After all, anyone with deep enough pockets could invest in setting up a new newspaper to rival the existing ones, and provide an alternative voice to those which were already making themselves heard. Creating a new national radio or television network, though, was until relatively recently a very rare event. The advent of the digital age, discussed in the introduction to this book, destabilised that argument, however, as new, digital ways of using frequencies meant a single frequency could be used for many more services than when transmission was purely analogue. Satellite television and radio, cable channels and video-on-demand services have served to multiply the opportunities to broadcast to wide audiences – as has the Internet, with its potentially unlimited capacity for websites and streaming audio and video services, and mobile phone technology with various kinds of apps for distributing content.

Consequently, the digital revolution has empowered individuals and groups with the opportunity to get their voices heard without needing the deep-pocket resources required to launch a newspaper. In practice, it is individuals or organisations situated on the centre-right and right wing of political debate that tend to have the resources to set up and sustain newspaper production, so it is generally more common for voices on the right of politics to be heard through the press, rather than left-wing opinions – as evidenced by the proliferation of titles published in the United Kingdom which are controlled by Rupert Murdoch, mostly supporting and promoting the interests of Conservative governments rather than of Labour (Starkey, 2007: 48–55). While the preponderance of right-wing newspapers skews the representation of political dialogue in the press towards the right, it is arguable that broadcasting regulation over impartiality makes broadcasting in general, and broadcast journalism in particular, much more fair in its coverage and the way it reflects the wide spectrum of political debate.

Despite the increasingly light touch, the legacy of the initially very tight regulation of broadcasting in the United Kingdom is clearly evident today. Both the public and private sectors are required to adhere to the *Ofcom Broadcasting Code* (2017), and the BBC has its own *Editorial Guidelines* (BBC, 2017) which its producers, presenters, journalists and independent suppliers must follow. Prominent in both of these online documents are requirements concerning 'due impartiality' during the course of normal day-to-day broadcasting and also some strict guidance over what are deemed to be election periods. Furthermore, actual legislation applies to broadcasting during election periods, in order to prevent broadcasters using their still-privileged access to audiences to try and influence the ways in which they might vote. The Political Parties, Elections and Referendums Act 2000 made some quite specific changes to the way broadcasters are required to deal with election candidates during election campaigns. The first rules laid down in earlier legislation were so tough they were often unworkable, but the requirement of successive Representation of the People Acts preventing any election coverage at all while the polls are open remains in force. That is why UK broadcasters cannot even mention election issues or candidates during the day of the vote itself.

These principles and legal requirements are taken very seriously by most broadcasters, and during the 2016 referendum on the UK's continued membership of the European Union, the BBC, for example, made very sure that every report from one side of the campaign was equally balanced, in terms of the airtime given to it, by a counterstatement from the other.[1] But here, as Chapter 3 examines, the fact of regulation does not mean that the BBC is free from criticism – its 'stop watch' approach to impartiality was widely seen as playing into the hand of the 'Leave' Europe campaign and allowing its proponents to make exaggerated or false claims unchallenged. This criticism aside, no such requirements are placed on the written press and many of the British newspapers indulge in not only straightforward partisanship, but also blatant campaigning for one party or perspective – often including denigrating the alternatives with misrepresentation and even outright lies.

The United Kingdom is not alone in imposing such well-meaning legislation and regulation on its broadcasters, and good examples can be found in Australia, Italy, France and Sweden (Starkey, 2007: 30–34). But it would be wrong to move on without noting that this is not always the case. A notable example of broadcasting being unconstrained by notions of impartiality is the USA, where such content regulation was abandoned in 1987 after much debate around claimed freedom of expression. Since then, in the relatively unregulated environment overseen by the Federal Communications Commission (FCC), rightwing 'shock jocks' such as Rush Limbaugh and even the later-to-become Vice President Mike Pence and others have achieved notoriety and considerable audiences for their on-air rants favouring Republican Party perspectives and denigrating the Democrats. On television, Fox News is well-known for favouring the right-wing perspectives of its proprietor, the same Rupert Murdoch as owns several British newspapers, while many suspect the National Public Radio (NPR) network of being 'liberal' in its outlook. In his first weeks in office, President Donald Trump frequently labelled CNN as 'fake news' and 'dishonest' whenever its reporting contradicted his own version of events (Slack, 2017). Paradoxically, in nation states which enjoy little or no real democracy, the broadcasting organisations are often part of the state and used unquestioningly as tools to reinforce and justify its hold on power. There is little, if any, room for dissenting voices or opinions in their output, and criticism of the regime is rarely broadcast – although this level of control in such countries tends to extend to all other media, including print and even public access to certain websites.

The resilience of broadcast journalism

In answering the question 'Why broadcast journalism?', it is also necessary to consider the alternatives. They include not only the written press – the oldest and, hence, longest-established, of the mass media – but also newer forms of communication that contribute to the metaphorical shrinking of the world predicted, but only partially described, by McLuhan (2001). Indeed, visitors to many of the various academic conferences on the relatively broad subject of media and communication in recent years might be forgiven for thinking that the established media had all but closed down, because of the frenzy of scholarly interest in 'new' media, consisting of websites, social networking platforms and mobile phone applications. In fact, audiences for the established broadcast media are in many countries as buoyant as ever, even if many academics seem to have forgotten about them. What follows is an attempt to paint a more accurate picture of a typical media landscape, generalisable to most countries in the developed world.

While the scarcity-of-frequencies argument inspired and supported throughout many decades and in many different countries the notion that broadcasting should be regulated, this has never been applied to the printed press, nor to exclusively online media. Regulation is a significant part of the distinctiveness of broadcasting, as where it is applied it has a significant impact on the media landscape. Firstly, though, one important caveat to this argument is necessary: the work of many broadcast journalists does indeed go online, as explained earlier, but its online presence is seldom the main focus of the endeavour. This has until most recently been a repurposing of content generated for the principal activity of broadcasting, and as such it is almost certainly of secondary importance to the broadcaster. It may, in being repurposed for online use, nonetheless conform broadly to the principles of broadcast regulation, even though it may not have to in that jurisdiction when it reappears on the largely unregulated Internet.

In many countries, the UK experience of the impact of the digital revolution has been replicated to a greater or smaller extent, but in essence it can be observed to have transpired in much the same way. That is, *print* has declined, while broadcasting has until now remained relatively robust in holding onto its share of the media market. It is important to specify 'print' here, because the press has also had to become – like broadcasting – adept at repurposing its content for online or mobile phone access in order to reach existing audiences in new ways and to find new audiences in order to survive. So the relatively cumbersome process of applying ink to paper, collating and transporting it by land or by air to retailers, often in millions of copies, has suffered from the increasing competition for consumers' attention from electronic media far more than has broadcasting. Table 1.1 shows the decline of 40% in total printed national paid-for daily newspaper sales in the United Kingdom in the ten years from 2006 to 2016. The newspaper industry has understandably been financially challenged by this, and has been struggling with a conundrum: whether to charge for the content it puts online, in order to compensate for the loss of paper sales, or whether to make it available free of charge online because there is so much other free content available there that readers might simply go elsewhere, rather than pay for online access to the newspaper website. Of course, as with the original print versions, the industry derives a substantial income from advertising placed around its online content, but the loss of both income and influence from the steady decline in newspaper sales has undeniably been significant, and by 2016 the response of one title, *The Independent*, had been to cease print publication altogether.

Over the same period, the overall audiences for broadcast media have fallen only a little, although there are clear signs that younger viewers are turning away from traditional television news bulletins.[2] The most pessimistic voices argue that the downturn in print circulations will inevitably, in due course, find its counterpart in a downturn in broadcasting. But for the time being, overall figures remain positive. In the final quarter of 2016, in the United Kingdom radio was still being listened to by 90% of adults aged 15 years and older (RAJAR, 2017). Those 48.6 million individuals were listening on average for 21.5 hours per week, meaning that – according to

Table 1.1 United Kingdom average paid-for daily newspaper sales

	February 2006	June 2016
The Sun	2,999,642	1,755,331
The Daily Mail	2,292,862	1,548,349
Daily Mirror	1,544,176	770,715
The Daily Telegraph	852,109	496,286
Daily Express	788,322	421,057
Daily Star	683,550	513,452
The Times	642,061	449,151
The Guardian	340,068	171,723
The Independent	229,162	No print edition
Financial Times	133,816	199,359
Total	10,505,768	6,325,423

Source: ABC.

the survey results – radio had their attention for a good deal of the time. Meanwhile, television was being watched at some stage in the week by 55.2 million people over four years old, representing 92.9% of the population (BARB, 2017). At the same time, however, there are signs that young audiences are migrating to new technology and platforms in the case of all three 'legacy' media – print, radio and television. Broadcast television channels seemed to have lost significant amounts of viewing to online video content providers, such as YouTube and Netflix.

Nonetheless, an average of 73.6% of the population was still watching broadcast television in some form at some stage in a typical day. As the newspaper sales data from the Audit Bureau of Circulation (ABC) in Table 1.1 concerns copies sold, and a single copy of a newspaper may be read by more than one person, a different organisation, the National Readership Survey (NRS), provides the industry-standard measurement of the actual *audience* for newspapers. The results, by comparison with broadcasting, were quite startling. In 2017 only 23.2% of the UK adult population aged 15 years and older – that is 12.1 million people – were reading national daily newspapers (NRS, 2017). There is, of course, also a smaller, partly additional audience for regional and local newspapers, but print is nevertheless far behind the broadcast media in terms of its overall ability to reach the available audience in the United Kingdom.

The newspaper industry might wish to contest the almost inevitable conclusion from the data discussed above that broadcasting has suffered less from the incursion of new media platforms and providers into the territory of traditional media. The most compelling defence of the press would be that they are no longer reliant on newsprint to reach an audience because their content is now available electronically and much of it is available online and via apps downloaded onto mobile devices. That is, of course, a persuasive counterargument but, as already noted, broadcasters also distribute

content in the same interactive ways. In the United Kingdom, the most popular websites of the traditional media providers include the BBC alongside
those offered by the newspapers *The Daily Mail* and *The Guardian*. Another
counterargument in support of non-broadcast journalism might be that the
audience data for radio and television include large amounts of listening
and viewing to content that is purely entertainment and does not constitute
news journalism.

That is also persuasive insofar as movie channels might broadcast only
movies, sports channels might feature only live or pre-recorded coverage of sporting fixtures and music channels might run only music videos.
Most radio stations devote the majority of their airtime to playing a mix
of recorded music and presenter chat, and some of them, although in the
commercial sector lighter-touch regulation still requires them all to broadcast hourly news bulletins, have cut the length of bulletins right back to
durations of ninety or even only sixty seconds per hour, in the questionable
pursuit of ever-larger audiences through a greater focus on music, rather
than speech, content. However, newspapers themselves do not publish on
their pages only content which can objectively be described as news journalism – as Murdoch's apparent predilection for topless models on page
three suggests. Between the news and sports pages, many newspapers find
space for content which is very 'soft' in nature if it is any kind of journalism, relating to celebrity gossip, fashion, shopping, motoring, travel, cooking
and so on, the print equivalent of some of the entertainment programmes
broadcast on mainstream television channels between the news bulletins,
and around which presenter chat on music radio stations tends to revolve.
Often, amongst the rest of their programming on television, music channels
broadcast slots for music news, movie channels feature movie news, and
sports channels include various forms of sports journalism – while talk radio
tends to encourage discussion of current affairs which displays similarities
with the comment, letters and leader pages of traditional newspapers.

It is worth considering here whether the migration of newspaper content online is another significant aspect of the trend for convergence noted
earlier in the case of broadcasting and other information and communication technology. In repurposing content for online distribution, are the press
moving into the broadcasters' territory by developing and publishing video
and audio content? Despite the presence of some high-profile video content
exclusives, research over a sustained period that compared multimedia content use on six mainstream UK and Chinese news websites in 2014 found
that in both countries multimedia content was very limited and that the
prevailing format was overwhelmingly text and still image – just as on the
printed page (Hao & Starkey, 2017). It seems that, for now at least, the use
of *broadcasting* codes and conventions in communicating journalistic content is largely still the preserve of the broadcasters, and that the press are
more keen to work online within the paradigms that have been their exclusive preserve for centuries.

One further significant advantage of so-called 'full-service' television channels, as opposed to niche channels which may focus on particular programme genres or repeats of proven favourites, is that they build large audiences with their general programming and then deliver to those audiences shorter, more concise news programmes at particular times of the day. In this way, broadcast journalism reaches much larger audiences than would be the case if its output were confined to the specialised rolling news channels, such as in the United Kingdom, on Sky News and BBC News and internationally on worldwide brands such as CNN, RT, CGTN, Al Jazeera and France 24. Music radio, despite its focus on music content and in many cases presenter chat, similarly delivers to the large audiences it is able to muster short bursts of broadcast journalism, usually at recognisable fixed points within the broadcast hour. Table 1.2 shows how in the UK market it is the mixed-content, full-service television channels that regularly achieve the highest audiences. During the period, the full set of BARB data provided on the organisation's website provided viewing figures for 316 channels (which were, of course, too numerous to include here, but the reach and audience share of most of them are tiny by comparison with those for the mainstream channels) as being less than 2% and in most cases either a fraction of 1% or even marked with an asterisk, which in BARB terminology means unmeasurable because of the limitations of the survey in sampling very small portions of the whole population (Starkey, 2004).

This dominant television audience share among full-service channels is an interesting phenomenon, and one which is particularly pertinent to understanding the nature of broadcast journalism today – and even, perhaps, in the future. Television electronic programme guides (EPGs) are not so difficult to navigate that viewers are prevented or discouraged from choosing to access rolling news from a dedicated channel at a time that suits them. Yet, because the biggest audiences for television news are to be found at early- and late-evening points in the fixed schedules of the more mainstream, full-service channels, it appears that the majority of viewers prefer their news to find them, rather than *vice versa*. The schedulers of such channels have traditionally worked on the principle that less popular programmes can be 'hammocked' between more popular ones, although television now being more fiercely competitive than ever may mean this has become too risky a strategy for some of them. The regular bulletins on the most popular channels, BBC1 and ITV,[3] were still – at the time of writing – scheduled at 6pm and 6.30pm respectively and then on both channels at 10pm. *Channel 4 News*, discussed briefly in the introductory chapter, ran at 7pm and the bulletin produced by ITN for Channel 5 was also scheduled at 6.30pm. BBC2 was the only such UK channel to exclude regular news bulletins from its schedule, on the basis that the BBC provides plenty of opportunities for viewers to access news elsewhere – although on weeknights it did provide a long-running and very well-established 45-minute news and current affairs programme, *Newsnight*, at 10.30pm.

Table 1.2 Television viewing data for the UK channels with the greatest audience
share, April 2017

Channel	Weekly reach (%)	Average weekly viewing (hours:mins per person)	Share (%)
All/any TV	92.9	22:50	100
BBC1	73.8	5:05	22.3
BBC2	51.3	1:17	5.6
ITV	54.6	2:49	12.3
ITVHD	15.82	0:37	2.7
Channel 4	49.8	0:59	4.3
Channel 5	44.0	0:53	3.9

Source: BARB.

Because not all news is of national interest, the two UK channels which
benefit from transmission systems that support regional variations to their
programming, BBC1 and ITV, both provided weekday regional news programmes in several editions according to how each network divided up the
country. In the case of ITV this regional demarcation relates to its historical
origins as originally a network of up to fifteen separate programme companies that gradually – as a result of loosening regulation over commercial
television ownership – merged into one large company covering most of
the UK except Scotland. The regional news programmes were scheduled
either before (ITV) or after (BBC1) the main national early-evening news
programmes, with short regional bulletins also being broadcast as opt-outs
from the national schedule in the early morning and late evening.

This pattern was well-established in many other countries, such as
France, where both TF1 and France 2 featured flagship 35-minute news
bulletins at 8pm and France 3 ran a sequence of national and then regional
news beginning at 7.30pm – even though there were several rolling news
channels available, including BFM-TV, France 24 and LCI. In the United
States, *NBC Nightly News* was running late-evening even though the network, NBC, also offers a rolling news channel, MSNBC, and a business
news channel, CNBC, both of which may be easily accessed by cable and
satellite viewers in the States. NBC's main competitors, ABC and CBS, also
had their own flagship news programmes, and the federal nature of the top
three US networks (meaning different 'affiliate' stations that opt in and out
of the national programming) also schedule local news before or after the
national feeds. The persistence of both public service and private sector television channels in scheduling news in such prominent slots in their schedules – many of them traditional slots occupied by news programmes for
many years – does suggest that, far from being a less popular programming
element that needs to be hammocked in order to sustain the kind of viewing
figures necessary to justify its existence, television news journalism can be
a peak-time blockbuster that actually builds some (often older) audiences

among the more general entertainment on offer. Arguably, it would not be good for democracy or for the intellectual well-being of a population if news and current affairs were sidelined or removed from mainstream, mass-audience channels altogether, and hidden away on niche channels or even abandoned completely.

It may have seemed at one time that the future of television – and perhaps to a lesser extent radio – journalism would be on instantly available but essentially niche rolling news channels. The launch of Cable News Network (CNN) by an American entrepreneur, Ted Turner, in 1980 led the way in demonstrating how a channel dedicated to continuous coverage of breaking and recent news events could operate on the basis of the constant refreshing and recycling of reportage and expert comment, and it was soon replicated by others. The presence of CNN's camera in Baghdad at the outbreak of the first Gulf War in January 1991, relaying the initial American-led air attacks on the so-called rogue state, lent a new impetus to the idea of a channel to which viewers could turn for instant confirmation or clarification of crises in domestic or world events. In the UK its imitators included Sky News, the BBC, with one channel for the domestic market, BBC News 24, and one for overseas, BBC World, as well as the ITV News Channel. Inevitably, though, the audiences for such content, which is normally essentially highly repetitive, are spread thinly over the now 24-hour news cycle, and so cumulative viewing figures are often disappointing. ITV News Channel closed down before its fifth birthday in 2005, having achieved an audience share of only 0.01% of the available audience. More recently, the BBC, faced with governmental demands for it to make savings on its annual budget, has merged its two channels at certain times of the broadcast day and resorted to more discussion-style programming in mid-mornings on the renamed domestic BBC News channel, in order to cut costs.

It is interesting that, in this market, Sky as a commercial venture has continued to invest in its inevitably loss-making Sky News, mainly because its presence on the media landscape makes a clear statement about the organisation's commitment to maintaining a service of hard news journalism, something it considers to be important because of its part-parent company's parallel newspaper interests. That may be unusual, given the normal preference of private-sector organisations for maximising profits at the expense of investment in content, as easily exemplified by the somewhat hasty exit of the newly-merged ITV plc from providing rolling news, just as – it could be argued – the format might have been on the verge of building audiences. It may be that, in many national circumstances, only the public sector would be willing to invest in rolling news, depending, of course, on the level of financial resources at its disposal, simply because it is not wholly motivated by the need to make a profit. It is worth noting that France 24, with its three channels in French, English and Arabic and a promised Spanish service to come, is wholly owned by the French government and paid for from the public purse, whereas any form of public-service broadcasting in the United

States is limited to the PBS Network, which because of the paucity of its funding has to rely on charitable appeals to its viewers to support it financially and certainly cannot afford to run a rolling news channel to rival the commercial channels, CNN, CNBC, MSNBC and Fox News.

Meanwhile, if some television viewing has made way for online content providers, both professional and amateur, and some radio broadcasters are finding Internet-only services such as Spotify and web radio stations nibbling at their audience figures, the newspaper industry also faces competition from lookalike newcomers onto the media landscape. Relatively new brands, such as the *Huffington Post*, have appeared and begun to challenge the dominance of the newspaper barons of the sector. The *Huffington Post* is regularly ranked in the Alexa[4] top 200 for web traffic, whereas most UK newspaper titles would, at the time of writing, have been pleased with a top 1,000 ranking. Other competitors include algorithm-based news-aggregators, such as MSN, that produce little original journalism but cherrypick content from other online publishers according to demographic data they can glean from IP addresses and cookies on their visitors' devices. However, a page view via an aggregator does not necessarily lead to a click onto the originating website, so making the content available to the aggregator might not be such a potentially lucrative decision by a newspaper. This means that for any media producer that relies upon text and still image for most of its content, and whose distribution platform is the crowded Internet or a mobile phone app store, the competition is particularly fierce.

In whom do we trust?

Since the availability of news from different sources has increased exponentially with the digital revolution, the issue of trust has become ever more acute. As subsequent chapters explore, broadcasters must maintain a level of trust if they are to survive the disruption wrought on the industry by social media.

Even discounting the availability of a cacophony of different voices on the Internet – in the form of individual and corporate websites, apps and social media, all clamouring for attention and making claims about events, trends, philosophies, geopolitical developments and so on – there are now so many public-facing sources which purport to be authoritative voices in the way that newspapers and broadcasters once monopolised. As a result, knowing whom to believe is a real issue for most ordinary citizens. The Pew Research Center found that in 2016, 81% of US citizens got at least some of their news from websites, apps or social media (Mitchell, Gottfried, Barthell & Shearer, 2016). Their news source preferences were as follows: 80% television, 59% online, 55% radio and only 26% newspapers. The domination of television is interesting, but it may reflect the easy availability of rolling news on the medium, whereas the decline of newspapers to only 26% has some comparability with the findings discussed earlier over the case of the

United Kingdom. Ignoring any concerns over partisanship, it can be argued that the three traditional forms of US media are relatively stable sources of information because of their mainstream status. There is consistency of control by press barons, light-touch regulation by the FCC, widespread affiliation to the main national broadcast networks and professional accreditation of journalism training institutions by the Accrediting Council on Education in Journalism and Mass Communications (ACEJMC). What then might be the stabilising influences, if any, on the rest of the news sources accessed online as the second-choice preference in that survey above radio and the press? They would inevitably include social media, although, at the time of writing, Facebook was struggling to respond effectively to growing concerns about its manipulation by purveyors of 'fake' news (Thomas, 2017).

As the United States elected in 2016 the habitually tweeting Donald Trump as its president, albeit by a quirk of the country's electoral college system in the absence of a majority of the popular vote for the maverick candidate, it can be argued that many of those alternative news sources contributed to a favourable climate for his election. Claims that US broadcasters played into the hands of Trump are examined in detail in Chapter 6. In the aftermath of the election, there were many claims of outside intervention through the spreading of 'fake' news and unsubstantiated rumours that were hostile to the Democratic Party candidate Hillary Clinton. Many of those websites, apps and social media sources provided just the environment in which such essentially undemocratic influences can easily spread. Some of the more popular web sources, such as the Breitbart News Network, are without parallel on the established media landscape, and as such a completely new phenomenon in mass communication – a development that is not universally perceived to be positive for democracy. According to the *New York Times*, the Breitbart website brought 'material that has been called misogynist, xenophobic and racist' right to the heart of the election campaign, when it would previously have been found only within fringe movements (Grynbaum & Herman, 2016). So influential in the campaign was the site perceived to be by Trump's opponent, Hillary Clinton, that she drew attention to it by expressing at a campaign rally her disgust at the right-wing nature of its content and the inevitable attacks on her politics.

The case of Breitbart News is used here as a mere example of how the digital revolution has opened up the once fairly stable and essentially very predictable public sphere of which Habermas (1989) once wrote, to the extent that it can become the mass media equivalent of the American Wild West. At the time of writing, the global Alexa rank for Breitbart was 237, but in the United States it ranked 47 (March 2017). Its rise demonstrates how in the new media age a business start-up can relatively cheaply develop similar editorial resources and structures to those of established media such as those in the newspaper sector, in order to develop sufficient content to begin to exert similar levels of influence on a country's democratic processes. This was made possible by the Internet being its principal distribution platform, rather than print, and the undeclared financial resources of its founders and continuing backers, who were solidly pro-Trump and anti-Clinton. It is impossible to say how many current and future Breitbarts might be out there in what is often termed 'hyperspace', but the potential for even more extreme examples beginning to exert influence on democratic processes in different parts of the world is evident – without any of the traditional sobering influences of dependence on the deep pockets of those who are able to invest in the newspaper sector and the stabilising influence, where it is effective, of regulation.

The moment to argue for content regulation of the Internet, if ever there was one, has probably passed long ago, not only because of the sheer scale of the sector as it has emerged and it will, undoubtedly, continue to evolve. This is partly because there never has been a spectrum-scarcity argument with regard to its development to drive a push for regulation, unlike over broadcasting when it was in its infancy. Similarly, the argument for the almost complete freedom of the press is one that is seemingly unassailable when it comes to suggesting that ownership of newspapers and some form of content regulation of their output might be appropriate in terms of promoting a fairer and more equitable public sphere within which competing ideologies might benefit from a more balanced environment. This was evident in the wake of the phone-hacking scandal in the United Kingdom, in which several newspapers were found to have broken the law in order to gain access to content involving celebrities and victims of crime that they considered their audiences would want to read about. One outcome of the official inquiry led by Lord Leveson during 2011–2012 was that the traditional right of newspapers to regulate themselves, through a self-appointed industry body populated mainly by newspaper editors, was seriously challenged (not for the first time). Previous threats by lukewarm critics in government that something would have to be done if the press refused to act responsibly over its content had gone ignored, including that in 1989 by the then Minister of State for National Heritage, David Mellor, that they were 'drinking in the Last Chance Saloon', and repeated controversies had resulted in the widespread discrediting of first the General Council of the Press (1953–1962), then the Press Council (1962–1990) and latterly the Press Complaints Commission (1990–2014).

There was by then quite an accumulation of evidence that self-regulation by the press was not sufficient to ensure it did not exploit its long-cherished freedoms in order to misbehave in ways that scandalised sections of the public and the establishment alike (Starkey, 2007: 64–67). One recommendation of the Leveson Inquiry had been that the press should be effectively forced through an amendment to the law on defamation to accept a mechanism which underpinned a new regulatory body through legislation: a self-regulatory body that would itself be regulated by another body given statutory legal powers to impose sanctions upon it for misbehaviour, and underpinned by a Royal Charter. The ensuing outcry from newspaper editors and proprietors was predictable, as they loudly bemoaned the end of democracy itself through a fatal blow being dealt by an authoritarian government to the traditional and hard-won freedom of the press (*The Telegraph*, 2016). Almost unanimously, the UK press insisted that any form of statutory-based regulation of their business would bring about an end to freedom of speech and seriously curtail the ability of the profession of journalism to freely investigate wrongdoing in government and elsewhere, to the inevitably gross detriment of the people.

What, of course, none of them was keen to admit was the irony of their position on the issue, when broadcast journalism had been subject to regulation in the ways already described since the BBC was incorporated under a Royal Charter in 1927. One of the claims that might have been made in defence of the *status quo* could, of course, have been that broadcast journalism is irreparably constrained by regulation and that neither the BBC nor the commercial sector of broadcasting in the United Kingdom is able to conduct credible and challenging journalism because it is cowed by the effects of regulation, as opposed to the self-regulation until then enjoyed by the press. Of course, such a claim was not made because it would have been palpably untrue. There may be a continuing vigorous lobby among the press for the size and scope of the BBC to be reduced, because it presents the press with some fearsome competition – some of the effects of which we have already observed in terms of falling circulations and buoyant viewing figures – but there is no contrasting lobby that claims that broadcast journalism is emasculated and needs to be given new freedoms to escape the metaphorical shackles of regulation.

Paradoxically, it is the written press that chooses to promote certain values, stories and perspectives according to its own partisan allegiances to governments or opposition parties, to lobby groups and commercial interests – to the detriment of other, potentially balancing values, stories and perspectives. It is the press that picks preferred outcomes at times of elections and referenda, using in many cases their front-page headlines, their choice of images and their editorial comment thinly disguised as objective reporting in order to attempt to influence the course of democracy. In the United Kingdom, that imbalance is normally in favour of the right, with few voices promoting left-wing perspectives – unlike in some other countries, where simply by happenstance the allegiance of the press may be more fairly distributed. In France, for example, both *l'Humanité* and *Libération* are aligned with the communist and socialist parties respectively (Starkey, 2007: 54–55).

One pertinent question is whether or not the various distortions of reality that seem prevalent in the partisan press and the unregulated Internet matter. There is a school of thought in mass-communication theory that contends in the 'effects debate' that people are in practice impervious to such distortions because they can naturally discriminate between truth and lie, informed comment and mere conjecture, fact and fiction. The dissemination of propaganda, its adherents insist, has no effect because people are not prepared to be influenced by it. There might seem to be some merit in this argument insofar as those people benefit from levels of media literacy that enable them to discriminate between content through a critical autonomy based on an understanding of the processes and motivations involved in making and distributing meaning through the various mass media. Some of this is acquired through experience of media content, as viewers or listeners learn to decode their codes and conventions.

For example, viewers do not need to see for themselves the process behind stop-frame photography in order to understand that a speeded-up sequence of the blossoming and then decay of a flower is not happening in real-time. Similarly, they understand that a sequence of *vox pops* is meant to reflect a representative cross-section of opinion on a particular issue. Depending on their levels of media literacy, though, they may not innately acquire a clear understanding that the letters published in a newspaper are only those which the letters editor perceives will meet the approval of the newspaper editor and, in turn, the proprietor; nor indeed that, as well as any instructions given to the editorial staff, a newsroom often fosters a certain culture, into which individual reporters become assimilated and the shared values of which then become regular influences on their work. In fact, the trend in the United Kingdom has been to tighten the national curriculum in schools to exclude media studies, to the detriment of the levels of media literacy among the population in an era when a better case for expansion, rather than marginalisation, of media education could be made.

So it is *broadcast* journalism, where regulation often demands impartiality, that can bring a welcome element of fairness to the public sphere. It is less easily hijacked by extremists and by hoaxers. It generally seeks to authenticate stories and claims made by third parties before disseminating them, although, as subsequent chapters will show, it is by no means immune from commercial pressures and mistakes. It employs journalists with appropriate training who are aware of ethical issues and strategies for dealing with them. It tends to set and follow high standards in responsible journalism, seldom being preoccupied with partisanship because to do so would be to invite criticism over bias, but striving towards impartiality in ways that can be argued to be consistent with democratic values. Perhaps most importantly, regulation imposes upon it codes of practice that will be enforced and may incur sanctions if those codes are broken. The importance of broadcast journalism cannot be understated, in an increasingly mediatised world in which ordinary citizens may lack sufficient media literacy to successfully navigate through the otherwise perplexing diversity of sources of information and comment.

How, though, does broadcast journalism operate in practice in its various forms, on television, on radio and online? Can it uphold this role in informing and supporting democratic debate? And how are these broadcast media coping with the disruption ushered in by social media and by ever-increasing commercial pressures? The next two chapters seek to address in more detail these issues in the context of the two most established electronic media of our age, television and radio. Both forms of media are seeking to adapt to change, as they exploit not only traditional transmissions using electromagnetic waves carried through the atmosphere to reach their audiences, but also consider how to embrace newer technologies and platforms to reach new audiences and bring new dimensions to their journalism.

Notes

1 See the discussion in Chapter 2 on the BBC coverage of the EU referendum.
2 See Chapter 2 for an analysis of news-watching trends.
3 The ITV *News at Ten* bulletin has, however, frequently been the subject of programming changes in an attempt to boost general audience ratings. This has led to the programme being referred to satirically as '*News at When?*'
4 Alexa Internet, Inc. is a California-based company providing commercial web traffic data and analytics. It is a wholly owned subsidiary of Amazon.com.

Chapter bibliography

BARB (2017) *Weekly Viewing Summary 27 March-2 April*. London: Broadcasters' Audience Research Board, www.barb.co.uk/viewing-data/weekly-viewing-summary/

BBC (2017) *Editorial Guidelines*. London: British Broadcasting Corporation, www.bbc.co.uk/editorialguidelines/ (accessed 2/3/17).

BFI (2001) *Northern Ireland: The Troubles*. London: The British Film Institute, www.bfi.org.uk/collections/catalogues/troubles/troubles.pdf (accessed 18/2/05).

Crisell, A. (1994) *Understanding Radio*. London: Routledge.

Crisell, A. (2004) 'Look with Thine Ears: BBC Radio 4 and Its Significance in a Multi-Media Age' *in:* Crisell, A. (ed.) *More Than a Music Box: Radio Cultures and Communities in a Multi-Media World*. Oxford: Berghahn.

Damome, E. (2011) 'The community of radio listeners in the era of the internet in Africa: New forms and new radio content, the Fan Club Zephyr Lome (Togo) as a basis for analysis' *in:* Gazi, A., Starkey, G. and Jedrzejewski, S. (eds) *Radio Content in the Digital Age: The Evolution of a Sound Medium*. Bristol: Intellect.

Grynbaum, M. and Herrman, J. (2016) 'Breitbart rises from outlier to potent voice in campaign'. New York: *New York Times*, 26 August 2016, www.nytimes.com/2016/08/27/business/media/breitbart-news-presidential-race.html?_r=0 (accessed 18/3/17).

Habermas, J. (1989) *The Structural Transformation of the Public Sphere*. Cambridge: Polity.

Hao, Y. and Starkey, G. (2017) 'Multimedia Journalism: A comparative study of six news web sites in China and the UK', *GSTF Journal on Media and Communications*, 3 (2).

McLuhan, M. (2001) *Understanding Media: The Extensions of Man*. London: Routledge (first published 1964).

Mitchell, A., Gottfried, J., Barthell, M. and Shearer, E. (2016) *The Modern News Consumer: News Attitudes and Practices in the Digital Era*. Washington, DC: Pew

Research Center, 7 July, www.journalism.org/2016/07/07/the-modern-news-con-sumer/ (accessed 17/3/17).

Ofcom (2017) *The Ofcom Broadcasting Code*. London: Office of Communications, www.ofcom.org.uk/tv-radio-and-on-demand/broadcast-codes/broadcast-code (accessed 1/3/17).

RAJAR (2017) *Quarterly Listening, October-December 2016*. London: Radio Joint Audience Research Limited, www.rajar.co.uk/listening/quarterly_listening.php

Slack, D. (2017) 'Trump to CNN: "You are fake news"', *USA Today*. Virginia: McLean, 12 January 2017, www.usatoday.com/story/news/politics/onpolitics/2017/01/11/trump-cnn-press-conference/96447880/

Starkey, G. (2004) 'Estimating Audiences: Sampling in Television and Radio Audience Research', *Cultural Trends*, 13 (1), pp. 3–25.

Starkey, G. (2007) *Balance and Bias in Journalism: Regulation, Representation and Democracy*. London: Palgrave Macmillan.

Starkey, G. (2014) 'Radio's audiences' *in:* Conboy, M. and Steel, J. (eds) *The Routledge Companion to British Media History*. London: Routledge.

Street, S. (2002) *A Concise History of British Radio*. Tiverton: Kelly Publications.

The Telegraph (2016) 'For hundreds of years, Britain's commitment to a free press has helped make this country a beacon of freedom for the world … But all this is now under threat from MPs and Lords', editoral. London: *The Telegraph*, 23 December 2016, www.telegraph.co.uk/news/2016/12/23/hundreds-years-britains-commitment-free-press-has-helped-make/ (accessed 17/4/2017).

Thomas, D. (2017) 'Facebook to tackle fake news with educational campaign'. London: British Broadcasting Corporation, www.bbc.co.uk/news/technology-39517033 (accessed 18/4/17).

2 Understanding television journalism

Introduction

Journalism, not for the first time in recent years, is mired in crisis. Disintegration of the twentieth-century business model, relentless cost-cutting and a dearth of original reporting have been accompanied by a crisis of confidence in elite media and a rash of 'fake news'. It is hard to escape the conclusion that the news business is facing one of its biggest challenges of the modern era. It is true that citizen journalists armed with little more than a mobile phone are delivering news we would never have seen before, stretching from the war-torn Middle East to terror attacks, domestic crime and protest on the streets of our cities. But user-generated content can also lead to a blurring of lines between fact and fiction, news and entertainment, the objective and subjective. In what is being labelled as an age of populism and post-truth society, where experts and facts can be wilfully overlooked, social media is becoming established as the main conduit for news.

So where does that leave television news broadcasters? Surveys and academic research outlined in Chapter 1 suggest that broadcasting in its broadest form is showing a measure of resilience when compared to the steep decline in newspaper circulations. But behind the comforting headline figures is a concern that traditional television news is being widely ignored and discarded by young web-savvy consumers who are increasingly relying on social media. Hendy even argues that the very word 'broadcasting' – transmitting programmes from a fixed central point of production out-wards to a large and dispersed audience – seems to be redundant in a less hierarchical network age where information flows freely in all directions (2013: 106). And as Helen Boaden observed in 2016 (2016) at the end of a 34-year career in broadcasting at the BBC, there is a danger that media is rushing very fast in order to stay still, with television news offering shards of information without the necessary context. Boaden, a former Director of News, argued that unless journalists slow down and make greater efforts to explain, "we may find that we are left with nothing much in our hands at all, except the indifference of an audience and a vacuous, unblinking, screen".

What then can television news do to ensure it enjoys the viewer's confidence and to guarantee its continued relevance in this rapidly changing media landscape?

This chapter starts by examining the broader trends in the news industry, focusing on the most recent developments in Anglo-American media after a year which saw Britons vote to leave the European Union and Americans elect President Donald Trump. It then examines in detail how these trends have impacted television news, exploring shifting viewing habits, the rise of politically partisan broadcasting and the prevalence of emotionally driven content in today's bulletins. Finally, the chapter investigates how the television news industry is trying to adapt to the new media landscape and whether there are still constants, underlying principles and values that can set it apart and ensure its survival in the future.

Journalism in crisis – the bigger picture

As noted in the introduction to this book, the political economy of media and broadcast technology has been in a constant state of flux for decades, and that can all too easily obscure the underlying purposes and practices of journalism, not least of which is holding democracy to account and good storytelling. But there is something about the current crisis in journalism that appears to have created a 'perfect storm' in which the doubts and fears about the very state of journalism run very deep. It started with the collapse of the advertising-driven business model that had sustained newspapers since the end of the nineteenth century; that in turn was followed by constant cuts to newsroom staffing levels and a reduction in the capacity to conduct original reporting; media companies are chasing online advertising with 'clickbait', and non-transparent algorithms increasingly dictate the news we consume, often confirming our own prejudices in what has become known as the 'filter bubble'. As a populist revolt against the political and media establishment sweeps across America and the United Kingdom, fake news has exploded onto the scene. Of course, there have always been deliberately false news reports and attempts to manipulate public opinion. But as Mark Thompson, former Director General of the BBC and now Chief Executive of the *New York Times* observes, "our digital eco-systems have evolved into a near-perfect environment for distorted and false news to thrive" (2016).

For Jay Rosen, media critic and professor of journalism at New York University, this is the darkest time for American media since World War I, when there was massive censorship and suppression of dissent (2017). It is worth recapping briefly how this state of affairs developed before assessing to what extent these developments are having an impact on television news specifically.

The roots of the current crisis lie in the combination of technology and economics, starting with the newspaper business as the Internet and social media sucked away traditional sources of advertising revenue. In Britain, after thirty years, 2016 saw the closure of *The Independent*'s weekday and Sunday print editions, one of the few liberal voices in an environment dominated by papers supporting the Conservative Party. Its demise (it exists as a website only) was for one of its former editors, Andrew Marr (2016), no more than a footnote in what he termed a "wave of creative destruction overturning all traditional media". In America, the *New York Times* has set itself an ambitious target of securing ten million digital subscribers (it currently has 1.6 million), and chief executive Thompson recognises that he is in a race against the clock to offset falling print revenues.[1] In its latest digital news report (2016), the Reuters Institute for the Study of Journalism suggests that these trends are not just confined to the Anglo-American media landscape, but rather make up a global trend, confronting publishers worldwide with unprecedented disruption to business models and formats from a combination of the rise of social media platforms, the move to mobile and growing public hostility to advertising (in print, broadcast or online). Across 26 countries surveyed,[2] the Reuters Institute saw "a common picture of job losses, cost-cutting, and missed targets as falling print revenues combine with the brutal economics of digital in a perfect storm". Business problems are becoming even more acute because of 'ad blocking', which ranges from 10% of news consumers in Japan to as high as 38% in Poland.

Against this background, the consequences for journalistic employment – and subsequently for original newsgathering – have been devastating. In the United States, the number of journalist jobs lost has reached such proportions that the American Society of News Editors (ASNE) gave up conducting its annual survey of employment levels in 2016, saying: "the structure of modern newsrooms makes it impractical and error-prone to try to estimate a total". This is, then, partly because the nature of jobs in the newsroom has changed so radically. But that aside, the ASNE had charted the decline of more than 20,000 jobs since 2006.[3] The picture is very similar in the United Kingdom, where journalist jobs have fallen inexorably by more than 6,000 in the two years to mid-2015. At the same time, employment in public relations has been rising. The result, according to former *Guardian* journalist Nick Davies (2008), is a sharp decline in the amount of original reporting. This has led in the United Kingdom and United States to what he has labelled '*churnalism*', a process by which journalists find it difficult to leave their desks, spending their time repackaging handouts from public relations agencies or news agencies. Core journalism and original reporting has, Davies maintains, been seriously compromised and weakened (ibid: 2). Currah goes so far as to say that increasing commercial pressure driven by the digital revolution threatens to 'hollow out' the craft of journalism, adversely impacting the availability of independent, factual journalism (2009: 5).

In a further twist, the news agenda is being increasingly driven by non-transparent algorithms, effectively dictating what appears on social media feeds such as Facebook and Twitter. The Reuters Institute for the Study of Journalism (RISJ) captured this trend in its 2016 review of the digital media landscape, saying that the choice of whether a story appears in an alert, a feed or on an aggregated homepage is increasingly decided by computer algorithms. That could take into account factors that might include how recent and popular a story is, what an individual reader has read or viewed before and what the reader's friends have been reading or sharing (2016: 13). It has often been said that consumers of news buy a newspaper in their own image (for example, right-leaning British readers may buy *The Daily Mail*) and therefore limit their exposure to different types of news or stories they might not otherwise see. But social media and such algorithms that personalise news – what Eli Pariser described as the 'filter bubble' (2011) – have pushed this to new extremes. As *The Guardian*'s former political editor Michael White explains, this simply reinforces what he calls our 'private ghetto', confirming our own established views and values (2016: 6). "Each of us," White says, "can live in our own streamed world without making much contact with rival versions of reality."

This new media landscape has spawned two further trends: the prominence of emotion in both the actual content and presentation of news stories and the proliferation of 'fake news'. It can be argued that the increase in emotion is partly attributable to societal changes and what Furedi (2003) calls our 'therapy culture'. We have seen this in television entertainment with the emergence of popular 'confessional' formats such as *Big Brother*. But emotion is now infusing news reporting, driven once again by digital media. To some extent this can be attributed to the rise of graphic user-generated content (for example, the spate of ISIS beheading videos) and the ability of such images to find their way directly into news feeds as raw and unedited material. Thanks to digital phone images and live streaming, we are now witnessing events live which we would never have seen before, from the Boston marathon bombing in 2013 to ISIS-inspired terror attacks in Paris, Nice, Brussels and London in the years since 2015. On the political stage, news coverage of the Brexit and US election campaigns has illustrated how the emotionally-laden personality has taken centre stage, a trend that has been emerging over the past decade with what Richards calls an 'emotional public sphere' (2007). Those two news events have also seen the emergence of what has been labelled 'fake news', stories which are either deliberately designed to mislead and manipulate public opinion or to generate advertising revenue (through 'clickbait') for websites masquerading as genuine news platforms. The concern has risen to such levels that politicians in the United Kingdom and Germany have started to consider ways of countering the phenomenon. The UK Conservative Party member of parliament Damian Collins, who chaired a House of Commons committee examining fake news, has gone so far as to say that it is a threat to democracy and is undermining confidence in the media in general (2017). There is no question that fake news stories were rife during both political campaigns but their impact remains at best unclear. An analysis by the news organisation BuzzFeed (2016) showed that in the final three months of the US election campaign the top 20 fake news stories generated more 'engagement'[4] on Facebook than the top 20 stories from established, genuine news outlets including the *New York Times* and *Washington Post*. A story suggesting that the Pope had endorsed Donald Trump's bid for the White House was shared almost one million times on Facebook. Despite this, it is far from clear whether there was any impact on the actual election. An analysis by Allcott and Gentzkow (2017) concluded that fake news in the election run-up clearly favoured Trump over his rival Hillary Clinton but dismissed the idea that it may have influenced the result.

So far this chapter has painted a very bleak picture of developments in the news industry. Indeed, for some pessimists, the changes wrought over the past decade, despite the proliferation of media, availability and diversity of platforms, mean the public is actually less well informed. The American sociologist David Altheide observes, for example:

> What governs our mediated existence are not facts, historical encounters with context, but rather emotional attachments, opportunities to express feelings, personal views and experiences that can be shared with friends … more information has produced little understanding.
>
> (Altheide, 2014: 5)

The dire warnings of our new media age tend to dominate professional and academic discourse but it would, of course, be wrong to paint an entirely bleak picture. News has also clearly benefited from social media and others place a different emphasis on change, maintaining that journalism will experience a renaissance, with the Internet providing access to more sources, citizen journalism delivering additional material and multimedia formats offering new means of connecting to an audience anywhere at any time (Allan, 2013; Bruns, 2003, 2011).

Where does this leave television news?

But where do these trends leave television news and has it also been sucked into a downward spiral similar to that experienced a decade ago by newspapers? Or can it remain resilient in the face of disruption and maintain public trust?

Certainly, the golden age of television news (if there ever was one) of the Reithian BBC or Walter Cronkite and the CBS Evening News is a thing of the past. It is inconceivable today to think of a television news anchor signing off with Cronkite's reassuring words "and that's the way it is", given the diversity of views and interpretations of the news available through social media. As Hendy observes (2013: 105), fewer and fewer of us are likely to see any point in having other people 'dictate' what we watch and hear. Is television news, then, as *The Guardian* columnist Stuart Jeffries (2016) contends, a "great sucking vortex wasting viewers' time" when they can get information faster and more personally tailored elsewhere? Or is there something enduring about the medium that means we still turn to television as a trusted source of news when a big story is breaking?

Audience analyses suggest that although broadcast television still plays a dominant role in society, younger audiences are no longer following this pattern and are in fact deserting traditional television news bulletins or 24-hour rolling news channels in favour of social media platforms. A survey by the Reuters Institute for the Study of Journalism (2016) concluded that viewing figures in the United Kingdom and United States have been declining by 3–4% per year on average since 2012. These declines are directly comparable to the fall in print newspaper circulations in the 2000s. The average audience for television news programmes is now actually older than the average readership of many newspapers. In France and Germany (even with an older population) the same trend is seen, with traditional television news bulletins declining as a source of news, especially for younger viewers. In 2015, the median age for viewers of Fox News in the United States was 67, MSNBC 63 and CNN 61 (ibid: 9). Highlighting this generational gulf in news viewing patterns, the report states (ibid: 3):

> There are no reasons to believe that a generation that has grown up with and enjoys digital, on-demand, social, and mobile video viewing across a range of connected devices will come to prefer live, linear, scheduled programming tied to a single device just because they grow older. This raises wider questions about how sustainable the broad public interest role broadcast news has played in many countries over the last 60 years is.

While the societal changes of a generation that has grown up with digital devices are clearly important, the trend is also being driven by constant improvements in technology as broadband speeds increase, devices offer higher resolution for online video and compression formats improve. The conclusion of the Reuters analysis is that television news is about to face disruption on a scale comparable to what newspapers have experienced over the past decade.

But arguably that is already happening. In a sense, change has been the only constant in the history of television news, starting with the dilution of the big network monopolies in the 1950s,[5] moving on to the emergence of 24-hour news channels with the first Gulf War in 1991 and the advent of social media in the past decade. Back in 1991, the CNN reporter Peter Arnett drew a global audience as he reported live from the Rashid Hotel in Baghdad when the first wave of US air strikes hit the Iraqi capital. The dim, green-tinted images of the sky, punctuated by the US missiles that represented the initial onslaught of Desert Storm, became a defining moment for CNN. The Baghdad telephone exchange was knocked out in the first strike but

CNN had a different communication system in place, allowing the network to continue broadcasting live. CNN producer Ingrid Formanek only later realised that they had a scoop and the wider significance of their reporting:

> We were the only journalists able to report. What I didn't realize at the time was that it was a global coup. News organizations around the world carried CNN's live reporting of the first night of the Gulf War I. That night made television history and catapulted CNN into permanent news prominence. From that moment on, live news coverage is what audiences demanded and news organizations strived to achieve.
>
> (Formanek, 2016)

'Live' was quickly to become the watchword for television news. A global audience tuned in to watch in real-time the second hijacked plane fly into the World Trade Center on 11 September 2001. And by the time of the second Gulf War in 2003, 24-hour Arab news channel Al Jazeera broadcast live from the conflict, crucially from the Arab – not Western – perspective.[6]

But less than ten years after that, at the height of what was optimistically called the Arab Spring, doubts had started to surface over the role of – or even need for – 24-hour news channels. During the insurrections in Tunisia, Egypt and Gulf States such as Bahrain, as in the Syrian civil war, video images of revolt, rebellion and conflict were posted directly by 'citizen journalists' (protestors or fighters) to social media sites. Their action effectively cut out the television news channels and spoke directly to the viewer. In 1988, when Iraqi dictator Saddam Hussein gassed his own population of Iraqi Kurds in Halabja, it took five days for the story to break in the Western media and for the first photographs to emerge. In August 2013, when Syrian civilians in the Damascus suburb of Ghouta were subjected to a chemical weapons attack, video footage was uploaded directly to social media sites within just one hour. It is this '*disintermediation*', cutting out the news organisation and going directly to the public, that has caused news executives so much concern. Many established television news organisations, such as the BBC, have invested heavily to embrace new media and user-generated content, incorporating external video content into their broadcasts and websites. But behind what is ostensibly an acceptance of social media, the BBC is keen to draw a distinction from the 'professional' journalism of its own editorial staff and to keep a grip on power. As James Harding, the BBC's Director of News & Current Affairs, observed in an address to UK newspaper editors in 2014:

> The news media are in danger of getting *disintermediated* as political spin doctors, corporate communications departments, pressure groups, celebrities and powerful people harness new technological platforms to speak directly to people. They are in the business of circumventing the media.[7]
>
> (Harding, 2014)

The root causes of the uncertainty surrounding television news are therefore very similar to those that have wrought havoc among newspapers a decade ago – a steady erosion of the twentieth-century business model and changing habits of news consumption driven by social media technology and the pervasiveness of mobile platforms allowing the direct access of video content online.

Some public-service broadcasters funded by the taxpayer, such as the BBC with its licence fee, have been partly shielded from the economic upheaval. Others, including new online challengers such as Netflix and Amazon Prime, have managed to build a strong subscription base, often fuelled by demand for premium sporting content (in Europe invariably football) or premium dramas such as *House of Cards* or *Game of Thrones*. But that hasn't really helped television news, and the 24-hour news channels are particularly exposed. They are costly and, with video going direct to consumers, they have lost their monopoly on being first with the news, with that honour often going to Twitter. As the BBC's former Director of News Richard Sambrook and Sean McGuire point out (2014), the infrastructure behind a 24-hour rolling news operation is impressive and formidably expensive – studios, anchors and a steady stream of contributors and guests (all ferried back and forth by taxi). They estimate that it can cost between £40–60 million a year to run a channel, and that for often very small audiences. The need to 'feed the machine' every news cycle (which can be as short as 15 minutes) has led journalists themselves to question openly the logic of 24-hour news. In one classic case, the BBC reporter Simon McCoy was sent to wait for a royal baby to be born at a London hospital. As the waiting dragged on, in some brutally frank comments he aired his frustration live on air, saying:

> Well, plenty more to come from here, of course. None of it news because that will come from Buckingham Palace. But that won't stop us…
>
> We'll just wait and see; it could be tomorrow morning if all goes well today … until then we're going to be speculating about this royal birth with no facts to hand at the moment.

The need to fill the airtime, or 'pad out' the airwaves with speculation and endless questioning of experts, has also led to accusations that the news agenda is being dumbed down or trivialised with the tag line *'breaking news'* much overworked. In 2006, Sky News, launched in 1989, famously won the race to cover a whale stranded in the Thames near London's Tower Bridge, sending up a helicopter for live aerial footage. The story ran for a full 36 hours. Of course, there have been genuinely important news stories that have been impressively covered: the 7 July London bombings in 2005 or Hurricane Katrina in New Orleans later that year.

News television, whether on the main network channels or their 24-hour rolling variant, has also quickly learnt the power and value of social media footage or user-generated content. In some cases, this has brought television viewers news they would otherwise never have seen. A holidaymaker's video of the 2004 'Boxing Day tsunami' was a case in point. But at other times, user-generated content has appeared to push the boundaries of ethics[8] and what had traditionally been considered suitable for television viewing. In 2013, an off-duty British soldier, Lee Rigby, was hacked to death outside his barracks in southeast London in an ISIS-inspired attack. The attackers, one with a bloody meat cleaver in his hand, had not fled but waited calmly for passers-by to take video and capture a statement[9] on mobile phones. An Independent Television News (ITN) producer sent to the scene quickly tracked down one member of the public with footage, brought him into the newsroom by taxi and loaded the video onto the news server. It had a 'scoop' on its hands that would beat the competition. The gallery played out the graphic and chilling footage onto the 6.30pm *ITV News London*. In the cold light of day, after the event, the television regulator Ofcom reviewed the incident. The footage had been broadcast live to those watching the teatime news, well before the 9pm watershed.[10] Ofcom received about 680 complaints against broadcasters who showed the footage, half of them about the first ITV bulletin. In January 2014, Ofcom ruled that the footage had not breached broadcasting regulations and was justified by the context and "unprecedented nature of the incident". But it did issue new guidelines on the need to give warnings before airing distressing content.

The broader trend in print journalism towards more emotional content has also been replicated in television news. The graphic nature of user-generated content – such as the Lee Rigby footage or the spate of ISIS beheading videos – is pushing the boundaries of what had once been considered fit for television viewing. Distressing images from the European refugee crisis or the civil war in Syria have brought human grief to our screens on an almost daily basis – in stark contrast to coverage of the 1991 Gulf War, when we saw sanitised images of US attacks almost as video games. Civilian deaths in Aleppo have been captured by citizens and the 'white helmet' rescue teams. The latter have been surrounded by controversy and accusations that they are part of an anti-Assad information war. There are also signs that such emotionally charged content is spilling over into the newsroom culture, fuelling the charge that rolling television news is heading towards 'infotainment'. In the wake of the November 2015 ISIS attacks on Paris, the veteran BBC journalist Graham Satchell broke down in tears during a live 'two-way' to breakfast television news in London. Speaking from the Place de La République the morning after 130 people had been killed in the attack, Satchell said: "The Eiffel Tower was lit up in red, white and blue, which, I think, is a sign of hope." On those words, he looked away as the tears welled up and had to walk off camera. The London studio anchors, and the viewing public, were full of sympathy for the reporter and the deeply distressing story he was covering. It was a totally normal human reaction for someone so caught up in the traumatic story. But at the same time, there is a sense by which audiences, as part of the therapy culture referred to at the start of this chapter, now expect on-screen emotions from their television reporters. The days of the detached, stiff-upper-lip reporter are in retreat; the television journalist is expected to have a 'voice' and personality.

Arguably such incidents make for 'good' television but they also bring into sharp focus a key question facing the television news industry: does it stick to the time-honoured principles of objectivity (detachment, impartiality, fact-based reporting) or are these practices and values anachronistic and in fact the very reason young people are switching off traditional news bulletins and the 24-hour channels? In the 1990s, the emerging 24-hour news channels broke the mould and shifted many viewers away from their fixed time appointment with the evening bulletin. But today social media and the rise of online video are challenging the *status quo* again.

If television news briefly found its way with 24-hour rolling news, it has certainly lost it again. It is hard to shake off the impression that some of those channels appeal only to bored businessmen stuck in overseas hotels or insomniacs. What then can television news do to remain relevant and how can it reinvent itself? And are the legacy broadcasters able to rise to this challenge or will the ground be captured by online video start-ups or third-party redistributors such as Facebook?

Can television news reinvent itself?

If the challenges facing television news are clear, the solutions are far less so. This part of the chapter examines the strategies and arguments being pursued by the established broadcasters such as the BBC, 'legacy' media with roots in the newspaper industry now moving into video, and the new generation of digital-only news outlets.

In Britain, as the established giant of public-service broadcasters, the BBC has found itself caught like a rabbit in the headlights. It is accused of a multitude of sins: of being an overpowering and bullying monopoly that has contributed to the decline of local newspapers; of applying its rules of impartiality so rigidly that pro-Brexit campaigners were given an uncritical platform to spread exaggerations and lies about Britain's prospects outside the European Union; of being part of a biased left-leaning media elite; of failing to grasp the new multimedia environment; or conversely of racing headlong into the scramble for instant news bites and 'dumbing down'. The long list of charges is indicative of the dilemma facing not just the BBC but many established broadcasters as they grapple with the questions of how to respond to the new digital landscape and seek to redefine a role for television news.

The reaction of the veteran BBC broadcaster Helen Boaden, cited at the beginning of this chapter, is to highlight the core values of impartial, accurate, fact-based journalism as an antidote to the tide of instant news, fake news and infotainment that marred Britain's EU referendum and US election campaigns. In a speech marking her retirement in 2016, she reflected on how the world of journalism she entered more than three decades ago had reflected a time of comfortable certainties. Newspapers, radio and television operated in their separate areas and were by and large well-funded. Now, of course, they are converging ever more and the public-sector broadcasters who once ruled the roost have their backs to the wall as they face an onslaught of competition (2016). Today, Boaden argues, television news sees things in 'shards', reporting quickly and fluently but rushing onto the next story without spending time to give context or to explore. She takes issue with the highly partisan coverage in the UK media of the Syrian refugee crisis in which some newspapers have cast refugees as villains, scroungers and terrorists – often referred to by media academics as the 'intruder' frame. She asks whether the broadcasters, and the politicians who appear in the studio, are being caught up in this rush to judgment:

> In our search for answers to a problem which appears if not intractable then complex, is the speed of the media's technology – and the politicians' willing participation in the 24/7 news cycle – obscuring rather than illuminating the issues?

> Are we simplifying the arguments if only by default, by not investigating them fully, or by appealing to an emotional response rather than an explanatory one?

These trends are being accelerated by the very digital technology that has made instantaneous reporting from around the world possible. It can at times mean that important stories such as the chemical weapons attack on Ghouta immediately come to light far more quickly than in the past. But it can also lead to a daily diet of 'breaking news' that is very ordinary and effectively devalues the currency. Boaden's plea is for what she calls 'slow news', a counterweight to the instantaneous news served up by algorithms fostered by Silicon Valley mantras of 'Act Now' and 'Just Do It'. This, she maintains, requires public-service broadcasters to hold to their age-old values of good journalism – impartiality, accuracy, expertise and evidence – and resist being pulled in the same direction as all the others. Equally, public-service broadcasters need to be aware of the imperceptible shifts in these values that can occur by contagion, taking their cue from other media and being swept along by technology.

Are these the wise words of a BBC 'lifer' who has a recipe for the future or are they the nostalgic remembrances of a past era when broadcast news journalism was in a cosseted backwater shielded from competition? Are these BBC values, and the established practices that make up the canon of twentieth-century objectivity, the answer? Or are they one of the very reasons why younger generations are no longer tuning in to television news?

The man currently responsible for addressing these questions is Director of News James Harding, a position Boaden herself held until 2012. Harding, who comes from a newspaper background, has also stood firmly behind the BBC's traditional values and even espoused the benefits of 'slow news'. And he has been robust in defending the BBC against criticism that its coverage of the controversial and divisive EU referendum in 2016 played into the hands of the 'Leave' camp by giving equal airtime – impartiality and balance – in news bulletins to politicians, economists and campaigners on both sides of the argument. The argument of critics is that the Leave camp indulged in distortions and lies which were given equal weight to the fact-based arguments of the 'Remainers'. A study by Cushion and Lewis (2017) found that the BBC was scrupulously impartial in the amount of airtime it gave to the pro-EU and pro-Leave campaigns. But aside from the narrow 'stop-watch' measure of impartiality, the study concluded that UK broadcasters generally privileged right-wing (mainly Conservative Party) voices on both sides of the argument, thus sidelining a left-of-centre case for Remain. Of 517 statistical claims made on news bulletins, very few were challenged by journalists or by independent sources. As a result, Lewis maintains that the news was dominated by tit-for-tat claim and counterclaim which was unhelpful for audiences trying to assess where the weight of evidence lay. But Harding is adamant that the BBC is not guilty of the charge of a false equivalence. Writing in *The Guardian* (2016), he made clear that journalism involves judgment:

> For the uninitiated: 'false balance' means thinking wrongly that you have to give pro and anti equal airtime, regardless of the facts, editorial judgment and the expertise of the interviewee. The BBC's rules are clear. We have to deliver 'due impartiality' and 'broad balance', terms designed to ensure that we are free to make judgments on the validity of stories, that we challenge facts and figures, that we acknowledge that different people speak with different levels of authority on a subject.
>
> (Harding, 2016)

Harding has also thrown his weight behind established values by announcing at the start of 2017 that the BBC would be establishing a team to fact-check and actively debunk deliberately misleading stories or fake news (2017). The 'Reality Check' dedicated team of journalists is tasked with examining stories that are being widely shared on social media. The BBC, Harding said, will be "weighing in on the battle over lies, distortions and exaggerations". The move can be seen in the context of a slew of quasi-journalistic organisations that have sprung up as fact-checkers, from Channel 4's FactCheck feature on its news website to measures being taken by the social media giants Google and Facebook.

At the same time, the established news broadcasters are also recognising the need for innovation. The BBC's move online in 1997 laid the foundations for its highly successful news website and in fact had a catalytic effect on other 'new media' (Hendy, 2013: 112); more recently it has put research and development funding into what it calls News Labs, all too aware that the big beasts of the newspaper industry, foremost among them the *New York Times*, where the former BBC Director General Mark Thompson is now Chief Executive Officer, are also moving into video-based news online. No stranger to reorganisation (his eight years at the BBC were marked by a string of job cuts), Thompson has embarked on a wholesale transformation at the *New York Times*, saying his goal is to increase its digital business fast enough to replace the declining revenues of its print division (2016). Although *The Times* has seen a strong growth in subscriptions since the election of President Trump,[11] the trend in print was clear – it still recorded a 16% fall in print advertising revenue while online advertising revenue, in contrast, rose by 6%. *The Times* now has a dedicated website *Times Video*, capturing news in video format and linking to the print story. While there is clearly no single recipe for success, other print giants are doing the same, such as *The Daily Telegraph* in the United Kingdom and *Der Spiegel* in Germany, the latter with *Spiegel TV*.

As the Reuters Institute for the Study of Journalism points out in its 2016 analysis of television news, incumbent legacy media face very different challenges to start-ups. The first, such as the *New York Times* and *Spiegel*, need to adapt formats and their production process to new platforms and new patterns of consumption. In addition to that, there is also a formidable gap to be bridged in the news culture between print and video. Although newspapers have been producing video since the early days of their websites, it had often been with low production values and of journalists talking about their already published articles. But the video now being produced has moved on, often featuring narrated clips of up to three minutes organised as an online 'channel'. The 'insurgents' or 'pure players' such as VICE News, however, face different challenges and need to create compelling content to build their brand (2016). Sometimes they have sought to feature longer-format video news, while also employing a distributed-content strategy by using third-party platforms such as YouTube and Facebook. By doing so, these news organisations are effectively recognising the power of social media platforms and the reluctance of consumers to move off those platforms. Al Jazeera has created an online news channel called *AJ+*, which runs across Facebook, Instagram, Twitter and YouTube in Arabic, English and Spanish. Unlike a traditional television news channel, *AJ+* has no anchors or hosts and its output tends to focus on social issues, sometimes with short documentaries that can run for ten minutes (although most are closer to one minute long). In 2015, it was able to record 2.2 billion video views on Facebook, half of those for thirty seconds, suggesting that the model of distributed content is finding favour with consumers. *NowThis News* has pushed the strategy even further by actually abandoning news on its website home page where a viewer is redirected to a choice of social media feed. Both *AJ+* and *NowThis News* emphasise how they tell their story in a way that suits each individual third-party platform rather than simply repacking exactly the same content.

Conclusion

This chapter has painted a picture of the television news industry in flux and experimentation. As yet, there appear to be no real answers.

The established television news broadcasters, whose evening news bulletins were for decades a shared and trusted source of information in the living room, know that their audiences are in rapid decline and are not capturing younger generations. It would, however, be unfair to say that it is all doom and gloom. Some habits die hard, and when a global news story breaks – most recently ISIS-inspired terror attacks in Nice, Paris, Brussels and Berlin – the instinct is still to turn to the BBC, CNN or one of the big-name broadcasters for live coverage. Equally, the big global set-piece news events, such as the Olympics or a presidential inauguration, can still draw a global audience (echoing the enduring power of what Dayan and Katz called 'media events' in their classic 1992 study of historic events). It is the one time when streaming video also gains traction online. There are signs too that in an age of fake news, adherence to normative values of fact-based journalism, impartiality and freedom from bias is enjoying a comeback, which, in turn, is benefiting the strong traditional news brands which can still generate a modicum of public trust. It would seem unlikely that the prime-time evening 30-minute news bulletin or 24-hour news format is about to disappear from our television screens any time soon.

But at the same time, it is difficult to see how such television news can in the longer term uphold its democratic purpose if an increasingly large share of the audience is turning to digital platforms. These traditional news broadcasters are being challenged to reinvent their ideas of television news not just by the pure video start-ups that are beginning to chalk up large numbers of viewers on social media platforms but also by newspapers with powerful brands such as the *New York Times*. Their task is made more difficult by the immense cost of maintaining such television news operations, declining revenues and, often in the case of public-service broadcasters, the pressure to deliver better – cheaper – value to taxpayers.

If they fail to tackle these challenges, they are likely to be viewed by an ageing and, ultimately, disappearing audience.

Notes

1 Advertising revenue at the *New York Times* fell by 18% in the third quarter of 2016.
2 These range from the United States and United Kingdom to the main economies of Europe and Asia.
3 See: www.poynter.org/2016/asne-stops-tryting-to-count-total-job-losses-in-american-newsrooms/429515/
4 The 20 top-performing false election stories from hoax sites and hyperpartisan blogs generated 8,711,000 shares, reactions and comments on Facebook (versus 7,367,000 for genuine news articles).

5 In the United Kingdom the ITV network was launched as a counterweight to the BBC in 1955.
6 See Chapter 7 for a discussion of global news channels such as Al Jazeera. Its rival Al Arabiya was launched in February 2003, just before the invasion of Iraq.
7 Speech to the Society of Editors annual conference, Southampton, 11 November 2014.
8 Chapter 6 discusses the ethical challenges in broadcast news journalism and explores in detail the decision to air footage of the Lee Rigby killing.
9 One of the attackers, Michael Adebolajo, said they had killed Lee Rigby because: "Muslims are dying daily by British soldiers…"
10 Ofcom defines the watershed as beginning at 9pm, saying that material unsuitable for children should not, in general, be shown before this time on television. It says unsuitable material can include everything from sexual content to violence, graphic or distressing imagery and swearing.
11 In the final quarter of 2016, the *New York Times* added net 276,000 digital-only subscribers, the best performance since it set up a pay wall in 2011.

Chapter bibliography

Allan, S. (2013) *Citizen Witnessing: Revisioning Journalism in Times of Crisis.* Cambridge: Polity Press.
Allcott, H. and Gentzkow, M. (2017) *Social Media and Fake News in the 2016 Election* (No. w23089). National Bureau of Economic Research.
Altheide, D. (2014) *Media Edge: Media Logic and Social Reality.* New York: Peter Lang.
Boaden, H. (2016) 'The case for slow news', *The Independent*, 29 September 2016. Available from: www.independent.co.uk/news/media/tv-radio/bbc-radio-director-helen-boaden-to-announce-resignation-at-prix-italia-preview-in-lampedusa-a7337181.html
Bruns, A. (2003) 'Gatewatching not Gatekeeping: Collaborative online news', *Media International Australia Incorporating Culture and Policy: Quarterly Journal of Media Research and Resources*, 107, pp. 31–44.
Bruns, A. (2011) 'News Produsage in a pro-am Mediasphere: why Citizen Journalism Matters' *in* Meikle, G. and Redden, G. (eds) *News Online: Transformations and Continuities.* Basingstoke: Palgrave Macmillan.
Currah, A. (2009) *What's Happening to our News – an investigation into the likely impact of the digital revolution on the economics of news publishing in the UK.* Oxford: Reuters Institute for the Study of Journalism.
Cushion, S. and Lewis, J. (2017) 'Impartiality, statistical tit-for-tats and the construction of balance: UK television news reporting of the 2016 EU referendum campaign', *European Journal of Communication*, 32 (3), pp. 208–223.
Davies, N. (2008) *Flat Earth News.* London: Vintage.
Dayan, D. and Katz, E. (1992) *Media Events – The Live Broadcasting of History.* Cambridge, MA: Harvard University Press.
Formanek, I. (2016) 'Operation Desert Storm: 25 years on', CNN, 19 January 2016. Available from: http://edition.cnn.com/2016/01/19/middleeast/operation-desert-storm-25-years-later/
Furedi, F. (2003) *Therapy Culture: Cultivating Vulnerability in an Uncertain Age.* London: Routledge.

Harding, J. (2014) Speech to the Society of Editors annual conference, Southampton, 11 November 2014. Available from: www.bbc.co.uk/mediacentre/speeches/2014/james-harding

Harding, J. (2016) 'A truly balanced view from the BBC: don't blame us for Brexit', *The Guardian*, 25 September 2016. Available from: www.theguardian.com/commentisfree/2016/sep/24/dont-blame-bbc-for-brexit-false-balance

Harding, J. (2017) 'BBC sets up team to debunk fake news', *The Guardian*, 12 January 2017. Available from: www.theguardian.com/media/2017/jan/12/bbc-sets-up-team-to-debunk-fake-news

Hendy, D. (2013) *Public Service Broadcasting*. Basingstoke: Palgrave Macmillan.

Marr, A. (2016) 'The loss of the Independent means the loss of a community', *The Guardian*, 13 February 2016. Available from: www.theguardian.com/media/2016/feb/13/the-independent-gave-me-some-of-the-most-exciting-times-of-my-career

Nielsen, R.K. and Sambrook, R. (2016) 'What is Happening to Television News?'. Oxford: Reuters Institute for the Study of Journalism. Available from: http://reutersinstitute.politics.ox.ac.uk/publication/what-happening-television-news

Pariser, E. (2011) *The Filter Bubble: What the Internet is Hiding from You*. London: Penguin Books Ltd.

Reuters Institute for the Study of Journalism (2016) Digital News Report, http://reutersinstitute.politics.ox.ac.uk/publication/what-happening-television-news

Richards, B. (2007) *Emotional Governance: Politics, Media and Terror*. Basingstoke: Palgrave Macmillan.

Rosen, J. (2017) 'Winter is coming: prospects for the American Press under Trump'. Available from: http://pressthink.org/2016/12/winter-coming-prospects-american-press-trump/

Sambrook, R. and McGuire, S. (2014) 'Have 24-hour news channels had their day?', Journalism, Media and Cultural Studies, Cardiff University [blog], 6 February 2014. Available from: http://www.jomec.co.uk/blog/have-24-hour-tv-news-channels-had-their-day/

Silverman, C. (2016) 'Analysis shows how viral fake election news stories outperformed real news on Facebook', BuzzFeed News, 26 November 2016. Available from: www.buzzfeed.com/craigsilverman/viral-fake-election-news-outperformed-real-news-on-facebook?utm_term=.pj79q1qGv#.hnWd7b7L1

Thompson, M. (2016) Interview, *Financial Times*. Available from: www.ft.com/content/5829e768-6a4a-11e6-ae5b-a7cc5dd5a28c

White, M. (2016) 'Balancing Act', *British Journalism Review*, 27 (4), pp. 5–7.

3 Understanding radio journalism

The senior service

It is more than a hundred years since a little-known Canadian inventor, Reginald Fessenden, first demonstrated how Marconi's use of electromagnetic radio waves could be put to more general use, by assembling a radio programme consisting of speech and music that might be of interest to anybody who could receive it (Starkey, 2007: 159). By the early 1920s, experimental radio broadcasts were beginning in many countries around the developed world, and private companies including Marconi's were by trial and error developing some of the world's first radio programming formats. Wireless quickly became the latest craze as early adopters of the medium proudly showed off the large box in the living room that brought distant, if often somewhat crackly, sounds right into the home. In the United Kingdom, the broadcasters struck a deal at first with the newspaper proprietors that they wouldn't broadcast news until the evening, so anxious were the press about the possible effects on their business of this new phenomenon (Crisell, 2004) – and so lacking in confidence were the broadcasters in not going ahead with daytime news in spite of the press lobby. As 'wireless' became better known as 'radio', and despite the many and varied technological and sociopolitical developments since then – for example, wars in Europe, Asia, the South Atlantic and the Middle East, the birth of television, the arrival of the Internet, the growing liking for media content on demand and the development of the podcast – radio has repeatedly confounded the regular dire predictions of some of its imminent demise.

Even the arrival in the living room of the television set in the 1950s failed to displace radio from the hearts and minds of its audiences, as listening merely shifted from the evening to the early morning and the daytime and from the home to the car and the workplace (Starkey, 2014). Radio became both ubiquitous and pervasive in the way the much smaller transistor receivers found their way into the kitchen, the bedroom, the bathroom and even the garden shed, with its linear diet of broadcast news, information and entertainment. Crucial to its resilience in the latter half of the twentieth century were the car radio and the clock radio, and now its new availability in this now highly-mobile and interconnected world means it is possible to listen via a laptop, a mobile phone or a tablet, making it one of the many different options on the daily commute to work.

The greater connectedness of today has brought with it new competition: people can now choose a much larger number of distractions on the bus or train that would previously have been restricted to the home, such as using a phone to watch a movie or surf the Internet, but they can also listen to a downloaded podcast which might have originated in a radio studio. The ubiquity and the popularity of radio have always presented radio journalists with a huge responsibility to get their reporting right, to exercise responsible and ethical decisions over their journalism, as well as to follow the industry codes and broadcasting regulations before the content they create makes its way into their listeners' lives. It very quickly became an authoritative medium in most countries, for all the reasons discussed in Chapter 1, and the expectations of its audiences have remained high. Because of the continuing importance of radio journalism, this chapter seeks to set it within a wider historical context by developing a brief historical overview of the platform, charting some of its high and low points, and then providing a further contextualisation and critique of the current practices that are typical of the profession, as exemplified in the commercial and public-sector radio newsrooms of the United Kingdom.

A little history

The Italian Guglielmo Marconi is widely regarded as 'the father of radio' (Crisell, 2002) because in the late-nineteenth century he perceived in earlier research by others into electromagnetic waves the potential for using the technology for instant communication over great distances. In 1897, he patented wireless telegraphy and continued experimenting with and developing different kinds of apparatus to improve the transmission of Morse code for the sending of messages through the airwaves from point to point. His wireless technology was first perceived as of use only for long-distance messaging, by shipping and the armed forces – who used it extensively during World War I of 1914–1918. When Reginald Fessenden first transmitted the human voice and music over the same electromagnetic radio waves, it was a major breakthrough in unlocking the potential of this new technology for mass communication. It was in 1920 that Australian operatic soprano Dame Nellie Melba gave a special concert in English, French and Italian and in doing so "demonstrated the power of radio broadcasting ... Her voice was heard throughout Europe and parts of North America, and almost sixty years of trials and experiments were at an end" (Crisell, 2002: 14).

By February 1922, the Marconi Company had begun broadcasting regular programmes of speech and concerts, as the father of radio began to monetise his invention. In October of that year, the British Broadcasting Company (BBC) was formed by a fledgling group of major wireless manufacturers, including the Marconi Company and the General Electric Company, with John Reith as its General Manager. Reith was to become a powerful force in the development of radio, the BBC and today's understanding of public-service broadcasting. His vision and core values are still at the very heart of the BBC and particularly its news output. Reith believed that the organisation had a great responsibility to serve its public in many ways and that it should be built on the three cornerstones of programming: to inform, educate and entertain. Daily broadcasts began a month later, using the call-sign 2LO to identify itself, and further services began to extend radio's reach.

> The company's appointees, led by Reith, to some extent followed their noses, making the broad assumption that the audiences shared their tastes … Gradually the *ad hoc* nature of programming gave way to careful planning, simultaneous programming between regional stations, and increasing centralization of output and policy making from the BBC's central base.
>
> (Barnard, 2000: 11)

There are parallels between the efforts of those early pioneers and the spirit of modern-day podcasting, which also developed as a spontaneous response to the development of new technology. The idea that creative people are making content that pleases them, much like artists, rather than simply responding to a commercial need or a brief that has been specifically designed with market research and data as its starting point, echoes these early broadcasts and offers this new form of sound-craft an appealing authenticity.

In those early days of radio, news – when it was broadcast – was unrecognisable from the 24-hour rolling coverage we can now access in many countries. In the United Kingdom, it was provided by news agencies, which were referenced at the start of every bulletin, and appeared only after 7pm. It was believed that radio news should *complement*, not *compete* with, newspapers, and Reith said: "I do not believe there is much demand for an earlier bulletin" (cited in Crisell, 2004). There was also the issue of cost. Speech-based programming is more expensive to produce than the playing of recorded music, and even in the 1920s there was plenty of music available to the broadcasters. Controversial subjects were also ruled out – a ban that would remain in place until 1928 (Barnard, 2000). This all changed in 1926 with the beginning of the ten-day-long General Strike, as workers in many UK industries, including the press, downed tools in protest at their pay and conditions. The absence of newspapers from the high street meant the BBC shed its original coyness towards daytime news and bulletins began to be broadcast nine times a day, filling the void as there were no alternative ways for people to access up-to-date news.

No more compelling a demonstration of the importance of broadcasting was needed and, following two governmental commissions investigating the nature of this new medium of wireless, the Sykes and Crawford

Committees led to the private-sector BBC being re-established as a public-sector organisation. In 1927 the British Broadcasting Company became the British Broadcasting Corporation under its first Royal Charter. The BBC remains bound by this effective promise of performance, which is updated and amended every ten years, most recently in 2017. It specifies the Corporation's priorities for news and other programming, its expenditure and every other aspect of its business. Today, commercial radio stations in the UK also have to abide by a similar statement of intent agreed with the regulator Ofcom during the licence application process. Any changes to the target audience, the music-to-speech ratio, the format or other significant amendments to their output must be approved by the regulator.

That original BBC charter of 1927 granted the BBC the right to gather its own news, rather than depend on news agencies, and it began implementing changes – initially by introducing a bulletin at 6.30pm – and over the course of a two-year period the total news output doubled. Hilda Matheson, appointed as Head of Talks, developed a style of writing that was more natural than agency copy when read aloud – being intended for the human ear, as opposed to the printed page, and therefore better suited for on-air use. A report she commissioned into the way the News Section should operate was "the most important document on news values ever produced for the BBC" (Hunter, 2000: 43). Sports commentary was also permitted, ending a practice that must have been frustrating for audiences and broadcasters alike.

> The absurdity of the restrictions was underlined in 1926 when BBC radio was able to broadcast live from the Derby. Listeners could thrill to the thunder of hooves, and the shouts of the crowd. But there was no commentary – and the audience had to wait until seven o'clock to find out who had won.
>
> (BBC, 2016)

In the early 1930s the autonomy of the radio newsrooms was increasing as they moved further away from the news agencies and printed press, and instead sourced their own stories and formed their own identity. From within the Talks Department there came a clearly defined distinction between BBC news values and 'journalistic news values' (BBC, 2016). There remains today a clear set of BBC *Editorial Guidelines* and an internal style guide that are available online for public scrutiny and are a useful resource for trainee journalists and students (BBC, 2017).

By the end of the decade, the news team had increased from six people to thirty (Crisell, 2002: 32), and newsgathering by BBC radio journalists began in earnest. The flexibility and immediacy of the medium was proven when a fire engulfed the exhibition centre at Crystal Palace and a young reporter, Richard Dimbleby, phoned in a report that took listeners directly to the scene of the action. The newspapers, of course, had to wait until the following morning to tell their readers their own account of the tragedy.

The 1940s were heavily dominated by World War II and its aftermath, and perhaps this moment in British history understandably marked the beginnings of an insatiable thirst developing among audiences for regular news, updated during the day. Bulletins had by then increased to nine a day and audiences of up to sixteen million were commonplace. Families would make an appointment to listen and sit together to hear the latest news interspersed between the popular entertainment programmes. The BBC historian Asa Briggs described the 9pm bulletin as "almost as sacrosanct as family prayers are said once to have been" (2000). It was during this period that BBC journalism earned much of the trust placed in it by its audiences, now a heritage that continues to benefit radio broadcasters across the Corporation and rival commercial newsrooms today. According to research by RAJAR, at the time of writing, radio remained the most trusted medium for news in the UK.

At that time, newsreaders started to be introduced by name. It was considered that although they had previously been anonymous, the listener would feel reassured by the personal contact of a trusted, named voice. There was some concern that all bulletins sounded alike because of the similarity of the speakers and their standard 'received pronunciation' accents, which could easily be mimicked to promote Nazi propaganda. This was indeed the case with the broadcasts of William Joyce, an Irishman who defected to the Germans and broadcast rival news bulletins on their transmitters aimed at the United Kingdom, earning himself the nickname Lord Haw Haw in the British press. So, in 1940 Wilfred Pickles became the first newsreader with a regional accent to read the news on the BBC. It is worth noting, however, that:

> Women were banned from reading news bulletins on the BBC right up to the 1970s, in part because early microphones were designed for the male vocal range and tended to make women sound 'tinny', but also because the BBC management believed that the female voice was too closely associated with gossip and lacked the authority necessary for news reading.
>
> (Shingler & Wieringa, 1998: 46, in Chambers, Steiner & Fleming, 2003: 29)

The period of the BBC's history lasting from 1946 to the early 1960s is the one Crisell notes as "probably its finest era" (2000: 74). There were now three national networks broadcasting a wide range of different content every day: the Home Service for spoken news, information and entertainment, the Light Programme for popular music and entertainment and the Third Programme for a more highbrow selection of classical music and talks. In 1957, the *Today* programme was launched on the Home Service as a 'morning miscellany' of news, current affairs and feature items. A far cry from the agenda-setting news focus of the current affairs programme of more recent decades, it was, in its infancy, a much lighter magazine format, with even a daily work-out routine for its listeners to follow. Even in the early 1970s, commented BBC World Affairs Editor John Simpson, no one accused *Today* of "dumbing down" "because it was pretty dumbed-down already" (Hodgson, 2014: 94).

The former presenter of the *Today* programme, Sue MacGregor, who made her name on it, recalled a disparity in assignments between men and women at the time:

> While ... there was no gender discrimination in the BBC pay packets, I discovered that not all the most interesting reporting jobs were evenly distributed. Foreign assignments and anything involving possible physical danger were handed out to the men in the team: rioting students at home or abroad, or industrial unrest, were not considered the province of women.
>
> (Chambers, Steiner & Fleming, 2003: 122)

The Swinging Sixties brought with them a cultural revolution and the introduction of pirate radio stations to the UK media landscape. Positioned in both the North Sea and the Irish Sea, a number of ships and former naval defensive towers began broadcasting a diet of non-stop music, news bulletins and presenter chat to a cumulative audience of millions of listeners on land, while remaining outside the reach of UK legislation prohibiting the use of unlicensed radio transmitters. The stations were enormously popular with teenagers, who had previously not been catered for, and it was impossible for the BBC to ignore them. The BBC's response was to rename the existing radio stations and add a fourth for young people, to be known as BBC Radio 1. The Light Programme became Radio 2, the Third Programme became Radio 3 and the Home Service became Radio 4. Radio 1 launched six weeks after the pirates were outlawed by new legislation, the Marine Broadcasting (Offences) Act, in September 1967. Its identity as a music station was undermined by an agreement with the copyright agency Phonographic Performance Limited (PPL) to play no more than eight hours of music per day (Barnard, 2000: 126). The pirates had been able to offer a full schedule of almost continuous music-based programming by not only pirating the frequencies but also the music, meaning that they weren't paying copyright royalties to exploit the tracks on their playlists. An experimental network of additional *local* BBC stations was soon declared a success, and it later grew in number to forty stations.

It was a promise made in the Conservative Party manifesto for the 1970 general election that eventually brought an end to the BBC's near monopoly on radio in the United Kingdom. The argument was that private-sector, *commercial* television funded by advertising had been introduced to the until then rather limited UK media landscape in 1956, in the form of Independent Television (ITV) and that, if a competitor to BBC television was already allowed, the same should be the case for radio. With the victory of the Conservatives under their leader Edward Heath, the initial plan for a commercial radio sector consisting of sixty local stations began to be implemented, but in time that number more than quadrupled (Starkey, 2015).

A further legacy of the post-war period came through a technological advancement that enabled reporters to go out 'in the field'. There was by then a well-established practice of 'voice pieces' being recorded in the studio by reporters to explain or add colour to a story, to then be included in a news bulletin. Most notable perhaps among examples of the genre was Richard Dimbleby's moving account of the liberation of the concentration camp at Belsen in 1945, which was considered to be so controversial it couldn't be aired on the nightly *War Report* programme. After Dimbleby threatened to resign, it was broadcast the following day. It was the first time the public had been exposed to the atrocities of the World War II concentration camps. However well-written and read to convey information about an event, these pieces were created retrospectively and consisted of carefully scripted, rigidly composed pieces. With the advent of location recording on magnetic tape using portable recorders, reporters were able to record more spontaneous accounts on location while an event was happening. There was some criticism of the sound quality of these 'as live' broadcasts; however, the then news editor, Peter Woon, was convinced that "if the journalist's reporting is really good, there is no substitute for hearing him say what he has to say".

Further developments in technology, including using landlines, satellite phones, mobile phones and the Internet, have enabled live reporting on location, and more recently connections using such platforms as Skype or FaceTime on TV and radio have been criticised and celebrated in almost equal measure ever since. There is no doubt that the latest developments in smartphone technology, even if sometimes the technical quality leaves something to be desired, have been transformative for radio journalists, who are now able to record, edit and broadcast not just voice pieces but more complex packages on location – particularly if they take with them a laptop – as we shall discuss in greater depth later in this chapter. In 1997, two years after CNN and Fox News in the United States, the BBC launched its own online service. Many commercial radio stations were much later to adopt this new technology, and later still to begin to understand its potential. Digital natives, or the generation often described as 'millennials', would find those early pages of rudimentary information and images to be laughable. Indeed, much online news at that time was simply radio copy that had been cut and pasted into the online template, with no use of multimedia, hyperlinks or other familiar modern conventions – and little or no attempt at rewriting the copy for its new context.

Regulation of radio

Since 2003, regulation of the UK commercial radio stations has been by Ofcom. This regulatory body is empowered by law to issue (and revoke) licences to broadcast, as well as to impose guidelines for broadcasters to follow and to ensure that those guidelines are adhered to. The current guidelines concern the output of local or regional stations – for instance, their commitment to an agreed balance between speech and music, the types of programming that the station will commit to broadcasting, and the range of different content for people living in the coverage area. On the matter of ownership, Ofcom has a duty to prevent undue dominance of the radio landscape in an area by any of the big radio groups, such as Global or its close rival, Bauer. There are also important guidelines for radio journalists to follow that sit alongside the law of the land, on privacy, for example, and most stations will expect their journalists to adhere to an internal style guide, which aims to promote consistency of style across their news output and must be followed or else large fines can be imposed.

The Ofcom Broadcasting Code is split into ten sections, with each providing guidance on what is, or is not, acceptable (2016). The first section is concerned with protecting the under-18s and gives a clear outline of what kind of content is acceptable for broadcast to an audience of under-18s. It also makes clear the responsibility the broadcaster has toward any participants in programmes who are under 18. It takes only a single complaint to lead Ofcom to investigate a claimed breach of the code, and the details of the subsequent investigation and the regulator's findings will all be disseminated later, online. If a station is found to have breached the code, the penalty could be a fine of several thousands of pounds. Typical complaints are around the language used in air, bias over issues of controversy and the appropriateness of content. Following the start of the 2017 BBC Charter, Ofcom is taking over some regulatory functions which used to be exercised by the BBC Trust. The BBC has its own *Editorial Guidelines* (2017), which relate to the work of journalists, including about appropriate content in news and programming. The BBC Trust also had additional responsibilities to oversee general BBC standards and finances, but an official investigation by Sir David Clementi into the governance of the BBC recommended an end to 94 years of self-regulation and concluded that Ofcom should assess both commercial and BBC content. The BBC *Editorial Guidelines* contain similar guidelines for journalists to the Ofcom Code, including advice on reporting crime, elections, privacy, impartiality and professional conduct. They are available online as a useful resource for staff and an interesting source of information for students. This chapter returns to the issue of regulation and the law, later.

A question of balance

As we discussed in Chapter 1, unlike in print and online journalism, broadcasters are required to produce balanced reporting over a 'reasonable' length of time, particularly in the periods preceding elections and referenda. Despite this being one particular strength of regulated broadcasting, there may well be an appetite in the UK commercial radio sector for radio stations to become partisan, rather than impartial. One of the arguments used might be that readers are able to choose newspapers that appeal to their views and social media users can engage directly with politically biased reporting. In 2016, Nick Robinson, a BBC political journalist and co-presenter of the *Today* programme, told an audience of Radio Academy conference attendees that he wouldn't be surprised if we started to see an emergence of left- or right-leaning commercial radio stations. Perhaps the management of the national Global speech radio station LBC were taking note, as they have a number of presenters who are partisan over various issues that they discuss on air.

The current regulations in the United Kingdom, and parallel legislation on the statute books, require broadcasters to be balanced in their coverage of the 'main parties', particularly during election periods or before referenda. However, this requirement of 'due' impartiality can be interpreted in different ways, and doesn't necessarily require equally balanced minutes of coverage for each party in any given day. Before the referendum vote in 2016, to decide whether the United Kingdom should remain in or leave the European Union, Ofcom and the BBC made clear that they intended reporters, presenters and producers to clearly understand what was required of them. During that campaign research conducted for this book sampled some of the coverage on the BBC and selected commercial radio stations. This was not an attempt to analyse every station at all times throughout the whole period, but it was simply a snapshot of the landscape during this period. From a range of news bulletins, discussion programmes and magazine programmes, the analysis was able to identify general trends and we were able to form some conclusions about the nature of the referendum coverage on radio and its possible effects.

Generally the research revealed quite strict adherence to the impartiality requirement. In the commercial sector, some presenters made clear on air their own voting intention – for instance, Julia Hartley-Brewer, who began an interview on Talk Radio with Nigel Farage, the characterful leader of the UK Independence Party (UKIP), by noting their common cause as supporters of Brexit, but clarifying for the audience that she would nonetheless be putting to him some 'tough' questions. Nevertheless, this amounted to more of an endorsement of his position than would seem to meet the impartiality requirement. Mostly, though, in news coverage on both the BBC and commercial radio, the research found that every point made by or for the Remain campaign was countered by a supposedly 'balancing' point – often of almost exactly the same duration. This act of 'balancing' the output would come in either the same bulletin or one shortly afterwards putting the position of the Brexiters, and *vice versa*. Global's LBC, a national digital station that is also on FM in London, and whose strapline is 'Leading Britain's Conversation', seemed to avoid a strict, mathematical interpretation of balance in the long period of political reaction following the Brexit vote, and adopted a more holistic approach across a whole broadcast day. Presenters on LBC were free to express their political values and challenge listeners on theirs, even though sometimes from totally opposite political viewpoints throughout the day.

As was the case in television, outlined in the previous chapter, the purely statistical approach adopted widely by BBC radio did little for the Remain campaign. The routine balancing act meant that the views of many economic experts, world leaders, business people or celebrities produced to support their case were dismissed. The manufactured 'balancing' response tended to consist of one of the Brexit supporters simply rejecting the case made by the experts, and often without any further substantiation. The former Conservative Secretary of State for Education, Michael Gove, proclaimed that "people in this country have had enough of experts" (Mance, 2016). If true, that would be a devastating blow for the profession of journalism of all kinds, because journalists rely on expert insight into specialised issues in order to substantiate their reporting. Often, indeed, balancing the opposing views of different experts is a tool to generate controversy and therefore interest in that story. Some presenters, notably on Radio 4's *Today* and on the teatime *PM* programme, did occasionally attempt to challenge unfounded or misleading assertions, but there was little attempt to scrutinise in any meaningful way the claims of either side, or to point out that there were natural imbalances in the campaign in that Remain had the support of the vast majority of economic experts. Often the BBC referred listeners to a 'fact-checking' service online, but its findings were rarely broadcast (Starkey, 2016).

It would be impossible to determine exactly how much the 'balanced' or partisan coverage of the referendum might have truly influenced the result, although there can be little doubt it had some influence when taken as a whole across the range of UK media platforms, both traditional and digital, social and professionally curated. In practice, news cannot always be a case of taking one side or another. Sometimes there are more than two sides to an issue, or the two sides do not hold equal weight. In the early 2000s there was a decline in uptake in the United Kingdom of the MMR vaccine for young children, due to coverage of a subsequently discredited scientific report linking the injection to autism. Although the claims were later disproven, and the majority of the medical profession was arguing for vaccination, the misleading representation of the issue as two equally-balanced arguments caused an outcry that discouraged many parents from allowing their children to be vaccinated and the number of cases of potentially deadly measles, mumps and rubella rose as a result (Starkey, 2007: xix).

Due to its public funding, the BBC tends to be more closely scrutinised than its commercial competitors. Particular criticisms came from the government in the 1920s and 1930s around the balance of reporting on the General Strike and Hitler's decision to leave the League of Nations. These criticisms continue to this day through a sustained narrative in certain parts of the press, criticising a perceived lack of balance from political reporters, particularly Political Editor Laura Kuenssberg over her reporting of Labour leader Jeremy Corbyn, complaints from Brexit-supporting MPs over balance around the prospects for the UK on leaving the European Union, and other issues around quality, bias and the BBC's budgets. The difficulty of achieving 'balance' all the time, and its being widely acknowledged, may be seen in the opposite responses such criticisms tend to provoke.

News hubs or remote control journalism?

In the pre-Ofcom era of radio regulation, when the Independent Broadcasting Authority began awarding local radio licences, stations were required to commit to a particular amount of radio news content in their licence applications. As the first stations were larger, relatively well-resourced companies serving coverage areas in large conurbations, they were usually considered capable of producing their own, autonomous, bulletins – mixing national and international copy and audio received from Independent Radio News (IRN) in London with their own, locally-generated content. A second and then subsequent waves of franchise awards introduced a number of medium-sized and quite small stations that were constrained not only in the broadcasting hours they were trusted to broadcast – some closing down in late evening – but also in terms of the autonomy of their newsrooms. In those early days, many stations were obliged to relay every hour the obligatory three-minute bulletin of national and international news supplied by IRN, and then to follow it with two minutes of their own locally-originated news, which they would have to present in as similar a style as possible to the national bulletin (McDonald & Starkey, 2016: 123–135).

There is now a considerably lighter-touch approach to the current broadcasting requirements for even the smallest of commercial stations, and this is due, in part, to the overpopulation of the marketplace that had developed by the late 1990s. The original plan for sixty Independent Local Radio (ILR) licences was soon forgotten and by the mid-2000s more than three hundred national, regional and local commercial radio stations were vying for the limited advertising income available. In some areas the stations were struggling to remain in profit and stay afloat in such a competitive marketplace. Various pleas were made over time to the regulator of the day, beginning with the IBA in 1984 (Stoller, 2010: 144–153), to reduce the amount of prescriptive regulation – including quotas of burdensome and costly speech output, ownership rules and logistical matters such as where content is produced. They argued that they could not afford, or couldn't prioritise, larger news teams at every station, so they were not able to fulfil the commitment to meaningful local news output.

Significant concessions were made by both the Radio Authority and then Ofcom over shared content and production practices within the large groups of stations that evolved through a series of acquisitions and mergers between the mid-1980s and the mid-2000s. This has been particularly significant for journalism, with the introduction of news 'hubs'. 'Hubbing' is where the news content for two or more radio stations in a group is created and/or broadcast from a single site, typically outside of the editorial area, while concealing the logistics of the practice from listeners in those editorial areas. As Crisell & Starkey observed:

> The first use of genuine news 'hubs' in this sense was in South-West England in 2002 when the previous regulator, the Radio Authority, was to allow the then largest commercial radio group, GWR, to experiment with a hub that served five previously quite separate stations: Plymouth Sound, Gemini FM (Exeter), Orchard FM (Taunton), South Hams Radio (South Devon) and Lantern FM (North Devon).
>
> (Crisell & Starkey, 2006: 20–21)

One of Ofcom's first policy documents, *Radio – Preparing for the Future* (2004), indicated the incoming regulator's intention to relax the regulations around news production, satisfying itself with the quality of the output rather than concentrating on the process of the production. This meant that as long as the output 'sounded local' it did not necessarily need to have been produced within that local radio station's premises. Modern production technology had made it increasingly simple for a station to sound local to its listeners, while coming from somewhere else entirely. Quite separately from hubbing, Ofcom also began to allow 'co-location' of whole radio stations in the same building – meaning one or more of those stations could be broadcast from somewhere quite far from its editorial area. Syndication of programming now allows whole programmes to come from studios far away, and Global has pioneered the syndication of large periods of the broadcast day from its headquarters in Leicester Square, London, to dozens of stations around the country – making a mockery of the original meaning of local radio. Stations are able to switch from local content to networked, pre-recorded or live broadcasts from another station in the group with such ease and such smooth transitions that a listener would have no idea that the news bulletin they were hearing on the hour had been pre-recorded ten minutes earlier by a journalist thirty miles away who had recorded similar bulletins, one after another, for a string of other stations all in the same hour.

One recent example was Newcastle-based Metro Radio, part of the Bauer group, which would collate and record bulletins for transmission on sister stations, TFM (Teesside) and CFM (Cumbria). Subsequently, TFM was co-located so that the entire station's output was broadcast from Metro's studios, despite local differences and antipathies between the two areas over their respective football clubs. Because in practical terms the only requirement on the use of news hubs is that a 'local journalistic presence' be maintained in each station's area, these smaller stations often have a single reporter servicing the area, gathering local content for the bulletins. The reporter will typically communicate with the hub newsroom in a phone-based morning briefing to agree which stories would be covered and also feed back to the hub on how certain events are being perceived by listeners in that area, suggesting additional local stories and then remaining in contact with the hub throughout the day. Practice varies across the various groups and across the regions. In some cases there is a reporter 'in the field' for only two or three days of the week, whereas in others there is a reporter present every day and the person undertaking that role rotates periodically so that team members can spend time in the hub, as well as time newsgathering. This can be a valuable experience for all involved, particularly for the location reporters, who can feel alienated from the dynamic of the hub-based part of the team and can find it difficult to progress in their career if they aren't networking with station management on a daily basis.

One of the frequent criticisms of hubbing is that the news output is not truly representative of news values that relate to the area being covered, and therefore does not meet the needs of the audience in the transmission area because the newsgatherers are not based there and they are not able to get a sense of their intended audience. Newsreaders based centrally also irritate locals with mispronunciations of place names, and while this may seem like a small issue, it undermines the integrity and authenticity of the output on what are branded as local radio stations. In fact, sounding genuinely local can be one of the strengths of local radio. National news organisations are frequently accused of being London-centric in their output and one of the deciding factors in moving much of the BBC's news, sport and programming output to a second base at Media City in Salford was to make people living in 'The North' feel that the Corporation was more representative of them. Audiences do have expectations of their local station which may not have changed since former journalist Linda Gage (1999: 58) claimed: "While a bulletin will cover international news, the listener expects a local station to present relevant weather and travel information as well as the local news – indeed, that is one of the strengths of local radio." Financial pressure may have persuaded the big groups to use hubs but, as well as its remaining a regulatory requirement, in most cases it appears those same groups still appreciate the value of even *perceived* localness (McDonald & Starkey, 2016).

One of the smaller commercial groups, UKRD, owns and operates fifteen local radio stations and takes a very different approach to newsroom operations, so almost every station has its own newsroom. After a short pilot, they decided to move away from the practice of hubbing and retain an in-house local news team at most stations, albeit one that consists of only two or three members of permanent staff. This means it is not unusual for a single member of staff to be responsible for the news output from 10am–6pm. As technological advancements have enabled more newsgathering through online sources, radio journalists are able to perform many elements of their job from the news desk. However, this poses particular challenges over breaking news or when a lone journalist needs to go to an important press conference or interview, and they have no option but to leave the newsroom unattended.

A journalist out of the office on a story has to keep a close eye on break-ing news and developments in existing stories, to ensure the pre-recorded bulletin left behind is not out of date or worse. Legal issues around reporting ongoing crime stories mean a criminal case can suddenly become 'active', and pre-recorded material that does not reflect that change in status could mean the reporter becomes in contempt of court. Local radio journalists in such situations are faced with a considerable challenge, in that although their news is local, in that it is being produced and broadcast locally by someone who lives locally, the bulletin may not sound as local as a hubbed station's output might without the freedom to get out of the studio. Journalists who are forced into an increasingly desk-bound role might often be forced to rely on audio from IRN to populate their bulletin, which would necessarily be only from national or international stories.

One UKRD radio journalist said the loyalty and sense of pride that local people have in 'their' station is an important factor in encouraging inter-viewees to come into the station to be interviewed, which saves the journalist from leaving the newsroom unstaffed. Whether the bulletins are produced at the station or not, there was a consensus among interviewees that the sta-tions should *sound* local. At one station where there were four journalists on shift, two of them were composing bulletins for other stations elsewhere while the station's own output was being written and recorded by another news editor 140 miles away. There is a difference, however, between content sounding local and being local. Among those elements of local news jour-nalism as first practised in ILR which tend to be absent when it is 'hubbed' are the 'on the spot' news reporter, the use of the news car, the reporting of court and council meetings, a permanent physical presence allowing pub-lic access, and above all one of the greatest qualities of radio, immediacy. Pre-recorded bulletins are difficult to interrupt with breaking news when one newsreader is servicing several stations. Radio editors talk about 'own-ing their patch' and winning the trust and respect of their listeners. With news journalism comes great responsibility, as the one who tells listeners if schools are closed when it snows, if roads are blocked or if power is down (Hudson & Rowlands, 2012: 37).

Radio journalism in practice: a typical day

Chapters 1 and 2 highlighted the radical changes to journalism wrought by social media, and radio has not been spared from the upheaval. In the United

Kingdom, jobs in the commercial radio sector have become relatively scarce compared with the days before news hubs were introduced and some are in many ways now very different. Indeed, changes in technology have ushered in changes in listening habits and in the practice of newsgathering. But for many radio journalists there are also a lot of similarities between what they do now and what they were doing ten years ago. Some newsrooms are more multiplatform than others, producing content for use online and on television, too. But many of the radio journalists interviewed for this book still saw themselves as primarily radio journalists, rather than multimedia or, more broadly, broadcast journalists.

Ethnographic and sociological research by Preston (2009) into newsrooms and their relationship with certain external institutions, particularly related to news-sourcing, found familiar set patterns of work that were echoed in the experiences of all of the interviewees. Many felt they were worked in a team, pulling together to meet time-based deadlines in a way that does not tend to be replicated in new-media newsrooms, which lack the regular hourly deadlines of radio. There were also clear differences between some of the stations researched – some simply opted into a national bulletin service overnight, provided for IRN by Sky News, and so the daytime news processes were paused overnight and had to be wound up again the following morning. This was done partly by using 'overnights', which are stories sourced and written by the afternoon 'late' team to be kept back until the following morning. These may be 'knock-on' stories, that is a development or angle that moves the same story forward for the breakfast audience the following day, or they may be based on embargoes imposed by external sources on all news coverage. These stories can be very useful to the breakfast desk editor who arrives at 5am and has the task of writing and recording 6am bulletins, perhaps even for four or more stations.

The first job of an on-desk news editor is to check the 'handover'. This may be done in person during a team briefing on arrival, or if there has been an overnight brief it would be via a handover note: a summary of the stories that have been run the previous afternoon, with a note of any audio that has been used twice and is therefore 'dead' (there are sometimes exceptions to this rule, for instance the announcement of Donald Trump's victory in the 2016 US election, although overuse of any audio diminishes its impact). The handover will also project forward, outlining the copy that has been provided for the breakfast team, together with its 'slug' (or identifier) and any suggested interviewees, with the status of any contact that has been made. For example, if the team are awaiting a call back from an interviewee, the morning reporter should not be in the dark about that contact, which would look foolish.

The editor would then either allocate newsgathering tasks to the rest of the team, or in the case of smaller stations would undertake them alone. A decade ago, the method of gathering updates from the emergency services was via *voicebanks*, a phone number that newsrooms could dial to hear recorded messages outlining the details of major fires or overnight crimes. They tended to be reserved for significant incidents and appeals for help. This practice has been all but eliminated by the widespread use of Twitter. Both a blessing and a curse for radio journalists, this does away with the need to sit through often lengthy voice messages that aren't ordered in terms of newsworthiness, so they could have to listen to something seemingly quite dull for twenty seconds before getting to the crux of the story and having to go back a second time to take notes. On the other hand, the general public also has access to Twitter and could have got the story directly, without the need for the journalist's intervention. As a result, reporters are immediately under pressure to get some added-value piece of information or interviewee to make that bulletin worth more to the listener than the tweet would be to a follower.

The next job is often to check the team emails for press releases or interesting messages and scan the social media sources. Applications like Twitterfall can be useful in aggregating tweets by geographical area or by key words. All potential stories would need to be verified to check their accuracy; however, there is a pattern of behaviour that tends to be seen more readily in local commercial stations, who have fewer resources to be able to verify the content, to use the 'retweet' function on Twitter to share a picture or video without owning it. They might use language that distances the station from the content whilst still being able to create an impression to the reader that they are 'covering it'. In times of great confusion, such as the terror attack on the 2015 Bataclan nightclub in Paris, errors can be made in a fast-paced and constantly moving stream of information. Then, a picture of the Eiffel Tower in darkness began to circulate, and was picked up by major news organisations and large numbers of social media accounts. The tweet caption attached to the picture indicated that the lights were out as a symbol of a country in mourning; however, it was simply the scheduled nightly switch-off. News organisations were forced to retract their coverage, to the detriment of the perceived trustworthiness of their output. The pitfalls and ethical challenges of the modern media environment are considered in more detail in Chapters 4 and 6.

The 'wires', as they are still traditionally known, remain a useful source of stories. BBC stations have used a package called ENPS as a way of assembling bulletins or programme running orders and sharing stories across news teams throughout the Corporation, while commercial stations use other software to do a similar job. Programs like Burli enable a group to share journalistic copy and audio across all of its stations, meaning they all have access to the same resources when a big story hits. They also benefit from the service provided by Sky News, which consists of stories that are written in a radio script format, often with audio. These scripts would typically be redrafted by the news team to fit their target demographic. Radio journalists, whether contributing to programmes, bulletins or other news content, have an acute awareness of the audience they are writing for, and this plays into decision-making at every stage from gathering vox pops to sourcing suitable interviewees, and writing scripts that are appropriate. Successful trainees and students of journalism listen to a variety of radio stations to gain a good understanding of the distinct differences and similarities in scripting between stations. The best scripts are written in a tone that suits the station as a whole and meets the expectations of the audience. They may even use cultural references that are applicable to that demographic or employ recognisable slang.

Critics sometimes refer to a 'dumbing down' of news, but it is important for radio scripts to be written in a way that can be easily understood on the first time of hearing. Listeners rarely rewind to listen again to a story, as they are usually doing something else at the same time. All radio copy should be succinct, free from clichés or 'journalese' and written for the ear. Peter Allen of the BBC's news and sport network, Radio 5 Live, commented: "Most writing is just too complex; too many sub-clauses; too much thought; too much trying to compress lots of facts into a single sentence. A sentence should have a thought in it, I think. Just one idea. Bump. Full stop" (Hudson & Rowlands, 2012: 119). Once written, the stories are arranged into a bulletin according to their newsworthiness. One of the challenges of hubbed newsrooms is that it can be difficult for the on-desk editors to properly understand the varied and nuanced audiences they're writing for on different stations. They also have to keep abreast of those stories that have the news value of continuity. In some of the newsrooms visited for this book, news editors were profoundly aware of these needs and that sometimes it pulled them in different directions. The reporters provided continuity in newsrooms where bulletins for their own stations were being provided by someone hundreds of miles away, while their own desk editors were reading and writing for stations elsewhere. Although these teams seemed determined to see the positives in the arrangement, and there were some, there seemed to be quite a heavy burden on each reporter, who is often the newest or least experienced member of a news team. It is worth noting that the confidence required to speak up in a news team environment, and having some certainty of understanding of the audience in the editorial area and how news values relate to them, are crucial skills new journalists need to acquire when in training on a journalism course.

In some stations, the on-desk editor reads the bulletin live, or pre-records it to fit a particular time slot. In others, it is handed to a presenter to read on-air. If this is the case it is important to have a good understanding of that presenter's speech patterns and prepare them for any difficult words or phrases. The key to radio scripting is to write for the ear, not the eye. It has to sound natural and be easy to understand, or when writing for someone else it adds an extra layer of complication. In reading a bulletin, there has to be a natural ease to the delivery so the audience doesn't feel as though they are being *read to*, but after that, style can vary widely. Some commercial stations apply a very informal style, occasionally using questions to draw the listener in to the bulletin. Such a script might begin as follows: 'What do you think of this?' after which an audio clip is played, followed by: 'Well, if you wouldn't like it, the chances are it can happen to you…' They are also likely to use colloquialisms and references to popular culture, such as: 'Check out the pics on Insta' in order to direct listeners to added-value content on social media, such as Instagram.

Most on-air reporters and newsreaders take a while to find their voice and become comfortable reading bulletins, and trends do change. Listeners value a combination of authority and warmth. Newsreader Kirsty Young said:

> You'll never be more than the story – neither should you be – but if people trust you, that's what counts. Look at Sir Trevor McDonald, who recently retired from the news. People find him a very trustworthy figure. They loved him. If he said it, they believed him.
>
> (Hudson & Rowlands, 2012: 311)

Radio journalists are often fairly transient people who tend to move from one radio station to another every few years, and frequently bulletins are read by journalists from outside the local area and consequently do not include any local voices. In the production of content, among the first ingredients a local news editor will remind new staff to include are local voices, stories and place names, in order to ensure that listeners feel that the local station really is for them (Hudson & Rowlands, 2012: 22). Representation of local voices was one of the motivating factors in the popularising of the radio phone-in in the 1970s (Starkey, 2015: 98) and it can be a powerful way of connecting with an audience and making them feel a sense of ownership and loyalty to the station.

A number of working radio journalists told of their dissatisfaction at centralised news provision, and there were two main reasons for it. The first was the common mispronunciation of names, which is annoying and can lead listeners to complain on social media. The second is a lack of consistency between the in-house team style and the outside provision. It can mean a large difference becomes apparent between a very colloquial, informal style at breakfast that includes 'banter' with the presenters, and a more detached, formal mode of delivery later in the day. While listeners may express a preference for one or the other they do not, however, appear to be unsettled by the lack of consistency that entails. The issue seemed to be more a matter of the professional pride of the journalists themselves. Elsewhere, this book's research found that, by happenstance, a newsreader in a hub had the local accent of one of the stations for which she was reading bulletins.

There is a noticeable difference between the process just described and the operation of news desks in public-sector BBC local radio. The emphasis for radio journalists in the commercial stations is largely, if not entirely, focused on bulletin production. They are working on a rolling cycle of hourly and half-hourly content that usually consists of a bulletin of just 60–90 seconds in duration, with longer bulletins at the middle and end of the working day. The BBC stations tend to be far more speech-based, particularly at breakfast and drive time, and delivering current affairs content on a daily basis for hours at a time requires a much larger-sized team of journalists. Here the research showed there were as many as five radio journalists at a station; however, only one will be working towards the bulletins. The others are sourcing content for the programmes, which could then be repurposed for the news bulletins. For example, a journalist may spend part of a shift calling an expert who might be able to contribute to a discussion on the drive-time programme, building a rapport through a telephone interview for some background research, and making plans for the expert to visit the station to take part in a live two-way conversation with the presenter during the programme. Short extracts, usually of around 15–30 seconds, would then be edited out of this live interview to enhance the bulletins throughout the rest of the afternoon, so that programmes and news are much more integrated than is usual in a more music-led, commercial station.

Radio talk

Interviewing is an essential skill and one that can help a radio journalist turn a somewhat unremarkable story into something really special. Although newsrooms may be short on time, under-resourced and under pressure from audiences and editors alike, there are precious moments during an interview when an interviewer is able to focus on that one person and what they are saying. Helen Boaden, until 2013 the BBC's Head of News, told a Radio Academy audience that during her time as a radio reporter she developed a reputation for making people cry during interviews. She added that the skill of a good interviewer lies in listening, and paying full attention to the interviewee. She said: "If you listen hard enough to people's stories, almost that genuine attention can be very emotional. At times, overwhelming. You have got all of this human emotion that only radio can do. Something very profound happens."

The great power of speech radio comes from those interactions that, when done effectively, feel to the listener much more like an interpersonal one-to-one experience than a mass media broadcast. It is much better being addressed personally than through a megaphone as part of a crowd. Listeners can be drawn in to the emotional breaking of a voice, or the smile they can hear on a very primal level, and making that emotional connection can result in a very profound moment. Often, adversarial encounters can have the most impact, such as when a Jeremy Paxman or a James Naughtie – both infamous presenters on BBC radio and television – take on politicians. But there are a great number of excellent journalists whose technique can be to sit and wait quietly, to tease a story out gently and allow the interviewee the space to tell the listener about their experience. Both techniques can be useful and effective in their own way and a good radio journalist, particularly a local journalist who doesn't have a specialist field, will have to cover a wide range of stories – unlike, for example, a financial reporter.

Certain topics are, though, taboo and it is up to individual stations or groups to interpret the Ofcom guidelines in ways that will best avoid a breach, with the possibility of a fine or worse. Many stations have lists of banned words and an appreciation of listener habits, expectations and values in order to give clear guidance to the news team. The research found one radio group has a strict 'no rape at breakfast' rule, which is designed to protect families from stories that contain sexually explicit details. This audience-led (or perhaps commercially-driven) approach to news selection and storytelling is an interesting discussion point, and one that has a unique place in radio because of typical listening habits and the ambition of programme controllers and, often, advertisers to encourage listening beyond the hour mark. Stories are presented in a way that one interviewee described as being rated 'PG on air and more explicit online', because audiences may actively choose to read the online versions, whereas they hear on-air bulletins almost by accident because they are, effectively, thrust upon them.

> The challenge of modern journalists is to find a way to negotiate the often-competing professional, commercial and ethical considerations involved in finding and presenting news, while adhering to a perception of journalism as playing an important role in society.
>
> (Burns, 2004: 7)

In what is a worrying trend, commercial interests are also impinging increasingly on story selection for radio. Some commercial stations visited while researching this book announced competition winners or on-air promotions within bulletins. Others banned the coverage of celebrities who appear on rival stations, and some came under fire from sales teams who were pressuring them to visit particular academy schools on exam-results day because those same schools advertise on the station. This pressure is not solely connected to commercial pressures on commercial stations, though. Even the BBC, which is normally very careful over even accidental product placement, runs charity radio-telethons under its own brands, Children in Need and Comic Relief – these provide national, regional and local coverage of donor organisations, many of them commercial, in return for donations to their various causes. This does not occur just in programming, but in news output as well. Of course, these events are heavily promoted as being for charity, rather than explicitly as being of a commercial nature. However, considerable publicity is given to many of those enterprises. Internal pressures such as these on news editors and their teams mean it is very important for incoming journalists to have a sense of their own ethical standpoint, to adopt a clear understanding of the regulations and laws surrounding their work and to have the strength and conviction to do what they think is right.

Chapter bibliography

Barnard, S. (2000) *Studying Radio*. London: Arnold.

BBC (2016) *About BBC News*. London: British Broadcasting Corporation. Available from: http://news.bbc.co.uk/aboutbbcnews/spl/hi/history/noflash/html/1920s.stm (accessed 3/3/17).

BBC (2017) *Editorial Guidelines*. London: British Broadcasting Corporation. Available from: www.bbc.co.uk/editorialguidelines/ (accessed 2/3/17).

Berry, R. (2014) 'The future of radio is the internet, not on the internet' *in:* Oliveira, O., Stachyra, G. and Starkey, G. *Radio: The Resilient Medium, Papers from the Third Conference of the ECREA Radio Research Section*. Sunderland: Centre for Media and Communication Research.

Briggs, A. (2000) *The History of Broadcasting in the United Kingdom: Vol 2. The Golden Age of the Wireless*. Oxford: New York.

Chambers, D., Steiner, L. and Fleming, C. (2003) *Women and Journalism*. London: Routledge.

Crisell, A. (1994) *Understanding Radio* (2nd edn). London: Routledge.

Crisell, A. (2002) *An Introductory History of British Broadcasting* (2nd edn). London: Routledge.

Crisell, A. (2004) 'Look with Thine Ears: BBC Radio 4 and Its Significance in a Multi-Media Age' *in:* Crisell, A. (ed.) *More Than a Music Box: Radio Cultures and Communities in a Multi-Media World*. Oxford: Berghahn.

Crisell, A. and Starkey, G. (2006) 'News on local radio' *in:* Franklin, B. (ed.) *Local Journalism and Local Media: Making the Local News*. London: Routledge.

Fleming, C. (2002) *The Radio Handbook*. London: Routledge.

Gazi, A., Starkey, G. and Jedrejewski, S. (2011) *Radio Content in the Digital Age*. Bristol: Intellect.

Hendy, D. (2007) *Life on Air: A History of Radio*. New York: Oxford Press.

Hodgson, C. (2014) *For the Love of Radio 4: An Unofficial Companion*. Chichester, UK: Summersdale Publishers.

Hudson, G. and Rowlands, S. (2012) *The Broadcast Journalism Handbook* (2nd edn). London: Longman.

Hunter, F. (2000) 'Hilda Matheson and the BBC, 1926–1940' *in:* Mitchell, C. (ed.) *Women and Radio: Airing Differences*. London: Routledge.

Loviglio, J. and Hilmes, M. (eds) (2013) *Radio's New Wave: Global Sound in the Digital Era*. London: Routledge.

MacGregor, S. (2002) *Woman of Today*. London: Headline.

Mance, H. (2016) 'Britain has had enough of experts, says Gove'. London: *Financial Times*, 3 June 2016. Available from: www.ft.com/content/3be49734-29cb-11e6-83e4-abc22d5d108c (accessed 20/4/17).

McDonald, K. and Starkey, G. (2016) 'Consolidation in the UK commercial radio sector: The impact on newsroom practice of recent changes in regulation, ownership and the local content requirement', *The Radio Journal: International Studies in Broadcast and Audio Media*, 14 (1).

Ofcom (2004) *Radio – Preparing for the Future*. London: Office of Communications.

Ofcom (2016) The Ofcom Broadcasting Code. London: Office of Communications. Available from: www.ofcom.org.uk/tv-radio-and-on-demand/broadcast-codes/broadcast-code (accessed 1/3/17).

Preston, P. (2009) 'An elusive trans-national public sphere? Journalism and news cultures in the EU setting', *Journalism Studies*, 10 (1), pp. 114–129.

Shapley, O. (1996) *Broadcasting a Life*. London: Scarlett Press.

Shingler, M. and Wieringa, C. (1998) *On Air: Methods and Meanings of Radio*. Oxford: Arnold.

Starkey, G. (2007) *Balance and Bias in Journalism: Representation, Regulation and Demcracy*. Basingstoke: Palgrave Macmillan.

Starkey, G. (2014) 'Radio's audiences' *in:* Conboy, M. and Steel, J. (eds) *The Routledge Companion to British Media History*. London: Routledge.

Starkey, G. (2015) *Local Radio, Going Global*. Basingstoke: Palgrave Macmillan.

Starkey, G. (2016) 'Regulated equivocation: the referendum on radio' *in:* Jackson, D., Thorsen, E. and Wring, D. (eds) *EU Referendum Analysis 2016: Media, Voters and the Campaign. Early Reflections from Leading UK Academics*. Bournemouth: Bournemouth University, www.referendumanalysis.eu/ (accessed 20/3/17).

Starkey, G. and Crisell, A. (2009) *Radio Journalism*. London: Sage.

Stephens, M. (2014) *Beyond News*. New York: Colombia University Press.

4   New platforms, new journalism?

Introduction

The US academic and media critic Jay Rosen is a passionate advocate of citizen journalism and has captured global attention with his redefinition of the traditional role of "the people formerly known as the audience" and the transformation ushered in by social media (2006); on the other side of the Atlantic, *The Guardian*'s former editor Alan Rusbridger has spoken fervently about the "mutualisation of news" where journalists and citizens come together in a productive social media environment (2009). Whether they like it or not, around the world, news organisations are coming to terms with a fundamental shift in the balance of power between those who produce the news and those who consume it.

   This chapter discusses the challenges and opportunities social media can offer broadcast journalists in newsgathering, sourcing and disseminating the content they produce. On the one hand, new platforms offer opportunities for the distribution and creation of broadcasting content. On the other hand, these platforms represent renewed competition for a share of the media 'voice'. The chapter explores the democratisation of the media which today allows ordinary citizens, who may have been excluded by the dominance of elite sourcing, to express their opinions and share their views on an equal footing with established mass media organisations (Knight & Cooke, 2013). It also discusses the potential pitfalls of such unmediated, often biased forms of mass communication and the challenges that poses for finding the 'truth' or in some cases for distinguishing fact from fiction. It will also touch on the evolving nature of the journalism content itself. The social media revolution offers more than just a series of technological platforms for driving traffic to an existing online version of a story. It can also develop spaces in which the story is shaped specifically to the platform, as is the case with Snapchat.

Relationship with the audience

Gradually, the relationship between broadcast journalists and their audience has shifted but never so rapidly as in the past decade. Forty years ago, correspondence was limited to viewers or listeners sending letters to the newsroom, usually fan mail or comments about the pieces they have seen or heard, or phone calls from people who thought they had a story that might interest the journalist. The introduction of email as commonplace in the 1990s increased the likelihood of that contact being made; after all, it is far easier and more gratifying to send an email that will reach the intended recipient in seconds, rather than a letter that will take days and likely go to a centralised contact rather than the particular journalist you want to reach. At this time, radio and TV stations began to include contact details on their websites as a matter of course and the channels between the parties became much more accessible to the audience. Also around this time comments sections were included beneath online news copy and readers were able to post their views. This immediate feedback was, of course, beneficial to journalists, editors and advertisers, who could tell straight away if a topic has sparked a level of interest among online users and could gauge what their readers thought about it.

But in the meantime, the use of algorithms has become so developed that the viewing and reading habits of the audience are beginning to exert a significant influence on news judgment. The phenomenon of what has become known as 'clickbait' is designed to drive eyeballs to websites and generate advertising revenue. For journalists, it has emphasised more than ever the economic value of content rather than its social worth – celebrity news can be financially viable because it generates a higher number of hits to the page than what might be considered more 'worthy' topics. This model can lead the business people behind a brand to be tempted to move further away from its ideological standpoint, or its positioning as a newspaper brand, in search of business. Further challenges facing journalists whose work includes space for comments include the hijacking of these feeds by people who have extreme views and little, if any, understanding of media law. A visit to any comments section below a story on Madeleine McCann will reveal all manner of libellous and speculative comments about the fate of the three-year-old girl who went missing from a holiday apartment in Praia da Luz in 2007.

Social media can, therefore, be a blessing and a curse. By the mid-2000s most newsrooms, and most journalists within them, were using social media for newsgathering, content distribution and connecting with the audience. As Gillmor (2006: 13) describes, the Internet brought with it new forms of communication and new opportunity for different ways of interacting. Society has moved from one type of communication to another. As Gillmor remarked: "The printing press and broadcasting are a one-to-many medium. The telephone is one-to-one. Now we had a medium that was anything we wanted it to be: one-to-one, one-to-many, and many-to-many." Further still is an added layer of communication, that of 'one-to-one-in-front-of-many'. Social media makes an even closer connection between journalist and audience member than the comments section does. It allows users to speak directly to the person behind the story, but it is also done on a public stage. This unusual dynamic is one that is rarely experienced in other public spheres. It is reminiscent of the occasional gleeful television reports seen of a pensioner in a high street publicly berating a campaigning politician whose ideas they oppose. It is their chance to finally say the thing they have been holding on to but never expected to have the opportunity to say. And they get to say it in front of an audience, which flatters the extrovert in many users; plus it is from the perceived safety of behind a keyboard, so they may end up taking it further than they would in a face-to-face communication. Journalists have traditionally held that same sort of distanced or hierarchical relationship with the audience as politicians. Although they come into their homes nightly and tell them information, it is rare that they would listen to the audience in return. Now that online users can speak directly to the journalists, they do it in a number of ways:

- The most valuable for both sides is if there was something in a report that the viewer/listener didn't understand. They are able to seek clarification and the correspondent learns that perhaps they hadn't been clear.
- Fan mail still happens, with users proclaiming their congratulations on the covering of a particular topic, and of course trolls are present too.
- 'Trolling' is a term given to online users who are overwhelmingly negative and often insulting. It is in many cases considered as a form of online bullying that moves away from questioning the professionalism of the journalist or the content they have produced and is more typically commenting on their appearance or a perceived view of their politics.
- This does not necessarily mean, however, that social media provide a democratic space where all users are equal. There is still an acknowledgment of the 'celebrity' status of high-profile newsreaders as they are frequently asked for retweets or shares to raise the profile of a charity or expand the reach of a topic.
- Audience members still reach out to journalists with story ideas, and they are arguably more likely to get a reply than if they send an email, because it is public-facing and the journalist does not want to be seen to be ignoring leads.
- Social media networks can also help journalists make, and maintain, an extensive network of contacts that lead to, and inform, the stories they broadcast.

The way a journalist interacts with other users shapes their identity, the perception of them by others, and this can shape their career (Quinn, 1998; Pavlik, 1999; Knight & Cooke, 2013). As such, it is important to state that many journalists have felt intimidated and threatened by the rise of citizen journalists, fearing that they would replace professional journalists. Gillmor (2006: 111) suggests a collaborative approach, accepting that "it boils down to something simple: readers (or viewers or listeners) collectively know more than media professionals do. We need to recognise, and in the best sense of the word, use their knowledge". The media landscape has settled into a pattern where user-generated content sits alongside professional journalism, sometimes complementing and sometimes competing. Online news content, whether on a news organisation's website, a blog, social media or other can benefit from its interconnectivity and draw of other sources through linked journalism, the effective use of hyperlinks, to the benefit of the reader. The BBC embraced the idea of empowering citizens through their iCan project in 2003 (Gillmor, 2006). The project encouraged activism and promoting change from the bottom up, using journalists to help citizens understand how to investigate or interrogate issues in their community and then report on their findings.

Dutch researcher José van Dijck (2009, in Hill & Lashmar, 2014: 155) uses a 'participation ladder' to divide users into six levels depending on their engagement:

- *Active creators* – people actually producing and uploading content such as blogs, videos or photos;
- *Critics* – which means they provide ratings or evaluations;
- *Collectors* – a term referring to those who save URLs on a social book-marking service which can be shared with other users;
- *Joiners* – people who join social networking sites such as MySpace or Facebook, without necessarily contributing content;
- *Passive spectators* – those who perform activities such as reading blogs or watching peer-generated video;
- *Inactives* – those who do not engage in any of these activities.

New platforms for distribution

The Reuters Institute for the Study of Journalism found in a 2016 report that 51% of people use social media as a source of news each week. More than a quarter of 18–24-year-olds say social media is their main source of news. This overtakes TV for the first time, demonstrating the importance of social media as an area of research for broadcast and online journalism scholars.

Social media offers an incredible opportunity for journalists to reach potential audiences. The nature of the retweet function on Twitter, for example, means that a user doesn't need to actively follow a news organisation in order for them to be exposed to its content; instead it can be curated into their news feed by a 'friend of a friend' system. This also removes the role of journalists as gatekeepers because ordinary people have access to some of the same primary sources of information. "In the past, edited and polished news products were traditionally closed off to the public; professional journalists in the traditional sense constructed the news … but social media allows for those gates to open" (Knight & Cooke, 2013: 4). They can see for themselves the police's Twitter feed for updates on a local crime story, or the Kensington Palace feed for the announcement of a royal baby, at the same time as the mainstream media.

This sharing of news, the ability to access what one might call 'accidental' users, opens a new world to journalists, who write attractive tweets in a way that is not overly onerous. They can link to the existing copy in their tweet without much extra effort. However, it is becoming increasingly clear that such users are often unable to differentiate between real and fake news stories and they retweet without engagement with the copy itself, relying more on the headline or caption than an understanding of the story. There is a danger, too, that because of the algorithms such sites use, the user gets more and more of a similar kind of content: that their views are repeated back to them in an 'echo chamber' scenario, rather than a space where beliefs are developed through engagement with ideas, exposure to informed counter-arguments and space to develop an in-depth understanding of news topics.

In short-form journalism, covering the day-to-day news, it is common for an online journalist to write their copy as normal, then tweet a link to that story. It will usually include a picture as a way of attracting the social media user's attention. The tweet should be concise – after all, it has to fit within the 140-character limit – and give an indication of the story content. Effective methods include lifting a controversial or attention-grabbing quote from the main body of the text to drive traffic onto the website. The pitfalls of this method, however, are that some users may only read the tweet and not the article, and this may draw attention away from the balanced body of the text and be shared by people with a superficial understanding. The tweet shown in Figure 4.1, for example, takes readers to a balanced report that contextualises the claims within a court case where the actor Johnny Depp is suing his former managers and they are countersuing. This context is important because it allows the readers to understand that accusations are moving back and forth between the two parties within a courtroom and they have not been proven true or false. Without the context, people who read the tweet would not get the fully balanced picture. Under UK law, words that are spoken within either civil or criminal court proceedings, that may be considered slanderous outside of the courtroom, are allowed to be reported under qualified privilege. This means whatever is said in court can be published as long as it is clear that these were claims made within a courtroom. If claims are made by the prosecution they may, at a later date, be disproven by the defence, yet all of the events can be reported upon.

Broadcast journalists working towards 'appointment to view' bulletins, or programmes, may use Twitter in the same method outlined above – to drive traffic to the news organisation's website where readers can see the package or interview clips before and after the main programme. They may also tease the bulletin by live-tweeting from an event. Taking a police press conference as an example, the broadcast journalist can tweet live updates to keep their users up to date with the very latest developments. In those

---

ITV ENTS News @itventsnews ·4h

Johnny Depp 'pays sound engineer to feed him lines', his former managers claim **https://twitter.com/itventsnews/status/859630489019273218**

Figure 4.1 Tweet reporting Johnny Depp 'pays sound engineer to feed him lines'
Source: https://twitter.com/itventsnews/status/859630489019273218.

Louis Theroux @louistheroux · 23 Apr 2015

Just been informed by Scientology lawyers that Scientology is working on a documentary about me. Little bit excited; little bit nervous.

Figure 4.2 Tweet by Louis Theroux promoting his film *My Scientology Movie*
Source: https://twitter.com/louistheroux/status/591240344051834880?lang=en-gb.

tweets they may promote the programme where they can flag the additional content they are working on. Viewers or listeners who want to be up to date with the very latest developments could also be interested in further analysis or discussion in the nightly programme, so the dual function of the live-tweets serves to both inform the user as an established and credible source of information as it happens as well as projecting forward to the analysis and additional content they will get from the main programme.

For longer-form journalism, for example documentaries, it is possible to build a buzz around the project while the project is underway. It is not uncommon to be asked to provide a social media strategy with a pitch to explain how you might develop a community of interested people who might not typically watch/listen to your programme, but might form part of an online community of people who engage with the subject matter. This can be achieved through the use of hashtags and the Twitter handles of interviewees or other key influencers in that community. Engaging content might include pictures of the interviews taking place or of interesting locations that were visited during the production, teaser clips or outtakes depending on the nature of the programme and, closer to the time of broadcast, the transmission channel, time and date.

High-profile documentary makers like Louis Theroux, whose *My Scientology Movie* was released at cinemas in 2015, would retweet articles written about the film, or about the subject, before and during the official promotion period. In the example given in Figure 4.2, he writes to Twitter followers as if they are friends. There is an assumption that they already know the project he is working on and that they are interested in the quirks that happen along the way. They are more likely to watch the finished project if they are invested in the process and want to see how it unfolds. This interaction is not just a cynical PR mechanism, it is for many broadcast journalists and documentary makers about community and shared interests as much as promotion.

New platforms for newsgathering and content creation

Since the arrival of the Internet, and long before they were labelled such, citizen journalists have also been able to disseminate stories. User-generated content is arguably at its most effective when gathered from within a major event. The 7 July bombings in London in 2005 happened at a time when mobile phone use was developed enough and common enough to have been the first thought of many caught up in the events. A modern-day first reaction: fight, flight, freeze, or phone. In a type of reaction that was unlike anything seen before, everyday people reached for their devices in order to document what was happening in the darkness of underground tunnels (where there were no news cameras to capture the suicide bombings). Prior to this, footage tended to be gathered after the event by people who were already filming and captured the events because they were rolling the camera, rather than taking an active, deliberate newsgathering role (for instance, Abraham Zapruder's footage capturing the assassination of John F. Kennedy in 1963). Due to the already widespread Internet connectivity of smartphones, citizens caught up in what became known as the 7/7 bombings were able to contact newsrooms to volunteer their footage in a way they had never been able to before. It gave a viewing experience that ordinary citizens could never have experienced – that of being inside the 'tube' station just after the attack. This has continued throughout the following decade, alongside other technology-driven cultural trends, like the selfie. In 2017, London was hit once again by a terror-related attack as a man drove a car along the pavement of Westminster Bridge to the Houses of Parliament, where he fatally stabbed a police officer. In the immediate aftermath observers again reached for their smartphones, with one taking a selfie at the scene. It was captured by another user and posted on social media, then shared among the online sphere and the traditional media as a representation/example of everything that is wrong with society. The ethical issues raised by such citizen journalism are discussed in detail in Chapter 6.

Similarly, the live Facebook streaming of the immediate aftermath of the shooting of Philando Castile, a black driver killed by a police officer in Minnesota in July 2016, was a turn of events that could not have been predicted twenty years ago. The idea that an ordinary person, in this case Castile's partner, could have the technology in her pocket to be able to video and stream live to the Internet via a platform that would save her content and allow it to be viewed live and on repeat around the world is today no longer surprising. It was picked up by mainstream news organisations, where it gained further traction, but is certainly among the establishing moments in Facebook Live's short history. What the mainstream media were able to provide to that initial, unmediated, confusing video was context.

Much like the 7/7 photographs from the London Underground, it needed explaining within the context of allegations of institutional racism among US police forces, a Black Lives Matter agenda and arguments around the ownership of guns. This was not an isolated incident, but one that is seen all over the United States. And while it can sometimes be difficult to establish facts, or they are provided by official sources (the same ones that are being criticised), this was an alternative angle. It could be used by a number of different individuals or groups to fit their agenda by packaging it in a particular way, but the raw footage could also be watched in isolation. This example illustrates that user-generated content can be both beneficial and challenging. The benefits of immersing the audience in the story, of deepening their understanding through footage that was gathered in the moment, or that provides access to a space that normal camera crews could not achieve are clear for all to see. Such material does, however, pose obvious dilemmas as outlined in Chapter 6. When information can be shared so readily at the touch of a button there is a clear tension between the imperative for established news organisations to be among the first, and for them to be accurate.

That aside, Twitter has in the meantime become a primary source of newsgathering for broadcast journalists. Where they would once rely on newswires and established contacts, they are now able to connect with the world from wherever they are working. Their contacts are further-reaching but the relationships still need cultivating. Software like TweetDeck and Hootsuite allow broadcast journalists to organise their feeds into specialist subjects by entering key words, hashtags or geolocational information. This separates the feed into columns from which the journalist can establish who is talking, about what subject they are talking, and where they are. Geolocational information can be particularly useful to local broadcast journalists, who will always want to know what their listeners or viewers are talking about – the 'water-cooler' topics that have engaged their audiences. The same technique is also advantageous in the event of a disaster where journalists are able to identify the legitimacy of tweeters' claims when they say they are close to the event. By changing the settings it is in fact possible for tweeters to change the location that shows on the tweet itself, so it may look like it was posted in Jakarta, Indonesia, when actually it emanated from, for example, Middlesbrough in the North of England. But the geolocational system can resolve this surface-level issue and show the true location unless a virtual private network (VPN) is being used.

By adopting established hashtags, a journalist can watch a story unfold, gauge public opinion on a topic, and be exposed to a range of useful opinions that might inform the story. They can also reach out to people who are connected to the story, either in a general way through the hashtag or contacting them directly via public tweet or direct message. Facebook has a slightly different opportunity via the group system. There journalists can find users who are connected by their enthusiasm for a particular topic and make contact with them online. Often journalists speak about making contact with people that would have been impossible or implausible in the physical world because their paths would simply not have crossed and these contributors can be very important sources of stories.

Verification becomes a priority

Many news organisations, certainly the large ones, have dedicated UGC hubs for verifying this footage and engaging with the people who share it. This often begins with their existing networks of contacts on social media – they know what their usual topics of discussion are and the locations they usually use to tweet. Then if those contacts share a video from nearby, the reporter already has a sense of the likelihood of its authenticity. But this alone cannot be trusted. The reporter must then track the origin of the video to ensure that it is not a moving image from a previous event being repurposed to fit the narrative of the ongoing one. If it was a video reported to be of an explosion in, for example, the Syrian city of Homs, but was really from an earlier blast in Aleppo, there are likely to be other copies online that could be efficiently cross-checked. The video quality might also help give an indication of its origin. If it had been filmed on a smart device, it would be more likely to have been captured live, whereas a very high-quality film might raise alarm bells that it was too glossy to be authentic UGC. If it passes this test and appears to be genuinely new self-shot amateur footage that matches the profile of the Twitter user who shared it, a broadcast journalist could contact the original tweeter and ask for details about where it was filmed. They would take another look back through the feed to see where/when the user's other photographs, videos and content were posted and the kind of content they included. They might even give a sense of the usual filming device so that if anything about the video being verified did not match, it would need to be fact-checked further. The broadcast journalist would then be able to trace the address and use tools like Google Earth and other maps to identify buildings or landmarks nearby that could be matched to the video they were attempting to verify. They might use weather reports from the day to check that it matched the sky on the video, or shadow patterns to establish whether the time of day was verifiable. If a piece of user-generated video matches these criteria, it is more likely to be used. Smaller newsrooms may not be able to fund UGC verification sections and will instead rely on either a centralised unit or outside organisations like Storyful, a News Corp-owned business concerned with gathering, securing permission for use, and verifying online content. Its parent news site boasts: "Storyful is the fastest and safest way to separate valuable content from social noise."

"You are fake news"

Donald Trump's infamous retort to CNN Senior White House Correspondent Jim Acosta's attempt to question him in the first press conference as President-elect in January 2017 cemented the popularity of the expression 'fake news'. The term, which rose to prominence in 2016, really refers to stories that are presented as news but, for the financial gain of driving traffic to a website that sells advertising or political manipulation, are entirely or partly made up. Since Trump's comment it has come to be an all-encompassing expression that moves from falsehoods written in a conventional news style to deceive the reader, through to stories that aren't deemed newsworthy, to anything that the reader just does not like.

Fake news sites often have web addresses that look similar to real news organisations, such as ABCnews.com.co, but the com.co is the giveaway. Real organisations will use .co.uk or .com. According to data gathered by BuzzSumo and posted on BuzzFeed, the top political fake news story shared on Facebook in 2016 was headlined "Obama Signs Executive Order Banning the Pledge of Allegiance in Schools Nationwide" with 2,177,000 shares, comments and reactions (BuzzFeed, 2016). Their research was based on stories that were entirely false, rather than partially so. Journalists and scholars often argue that the foundation stones of professional journalism remain firmly in place despite the rise of alternative sources, user-generated content and availability of primary sources. These include fact-checking, but this does not mean that fake stories do not slip through the net. In April 2017, a fake news story was picked up by mainstream media in the United Kingdom and United States about a married couple who found out during routine DNA tests that they were twins. The story was published on major newspaper websites, including the *Daily Mail*, *Mirror* and *Sun* websites in the United Kingdom. The original source was cited as the *Mississippi Herald*, a website-only publication that had no posts before 11 April. Online teams who are clearly failing to check the legitimacy of such stories before publishing them risk undermining the audience trust in the publication. In fact, some of the most effective fake news stories are ones that seem feasible or that have a convincing mixture of true and false information. Of course, this is not an entirely new phenomenon; indeed, one of the most famous cases of fake news was that written by former *New York Times* reporter Jayson Blair, who was found to have plagiarised and invented stories before his resignation from the paper in 2003. The motivating factor for Blair's misdeeds is unknown; however, the mainspring of much of the online fake news we have seen in the last two years is to drive traffic to advertising on websites, thus generating revenue – the very clickbait mentioned in the examples given above.

Predictions for the changing face of online journalism for 2017 and beyond often focus on the role to be played by fact-checking services. As Trump became ever closer to the presidency, many sites, including factcheck.org and politifact.com as well as the *Washington Post*, *The Guardian* and the BBC, provided real-time and retrospective fact-checking to accompany his speeches. In December 2016, *The Washington Post* launched a Chrome browser plug-in that provided commentary on Trump's tweets, a move that has the potential to provide useful context. But at the same time, it has been criticised as a 'far-left' move and 'preaching to the choir' as people who are likely to install the plug-in are searching for the alternative narrative, whereas others who are politically aligned to Trump are naturally more accepting of his political message and would therefore be less likely to install. As newspapers are privately owned, they tend to have a clear political standpoint, and when it comes to fact-checking they are frequently dismissed when they offer an alternative political viewpoint to the reader's own. Since broadcasters in the United Kingdom are bound by clear regulations on impartiality, they are read as more politically neutral by their users and therefore trust in them as providers of balanced news is higher. This is not the case in the United States, where partisan political coverage by major broadcasters is commonplace.

News values and blurred lines

Scholars of journalism will be familiar with the concept of news values (Galtung & Ruge, 1965; Harcup & O'Neill, 2001). But the focus of this section is on the value of news, rather than the values possessed by a story in terms of its newsworthiness. By this is meant the financial, social and cultural value to a democratic society.

Mitchell Stephens writes, when discussing coverage of the 2012 US Supreme Court's decision on the 'Obamacare' bill that roughly twenty hours after the event had broken on the SCOTUSblog (Supreme Court of the United States), on rolling TV channels, Twitter and online, leading newspapers still printed the news as if it was new. He asked:

> Did they think their readers hadn't already learned this news? … Did they feel some obligation to record this momentous event for history – even though history is now being recorded on the Web … My guess is that many of our journalists are simply stuck in an out-dated paradigm.
>
> (Stephens, 2014)

Of course, it is true that print has lost any immediacy it ever had. This has been the case for decades, ever since radio arrived with its comparatively easily transportable broadcasting systems and programming that could be easily interrupted to make way for big news stories. The trend has continued unabated since then, through the rise of 24-hour rolling news channels on radio and TV and the arrival of the Internet, social media, 4G and smart devices. There is no doubt that, when it comes to speed, newspapers are going to lose every time. What they have in their favour over the non-professional bloggers and social media users is expertise. They have the space to reflect, analyse and investigate. This, however, is expensive and increasingly difficult as costs, and staffing levels, are cut. Nowhere was the danger to journalistic standards better illustrated than during a police manhunt in the North of England in 2010, when some smaller broadcasters relied heavily on Twitter to cover what would otherwise have been a very expensive story. Raoul Moat had been out of prison for just two days before shooting his ex-girlfriend and killing her partner. He threatened police during phone calls to 999 and shot a traffic officer in the face, permanently blinding him, before going on the run for six days. During that time there were numerous sightings of Moat before police confirmed that he was believed to be in the small Northumberland town of Rothbury. Schools were on lockdown, armed police and military resources were dispatched to assist. By this time the national news media had joined their local counterparts and there was a huge public interest in the story. On the night of 9 July, events escalated as an armed Moat was in a stand-off with police. Some local and regional radio stations immediately mobilised staff to go to the scene, while others continued with automated programming and the national IRN feed because they did not have the resources to manage anything close to rolling coverage. While the rolling TV news channels had a continuous feed from journalists at the scene and their experts in the studio, reporters feeding into traditional news programmes had to wait until their scheduled slot. They built interest in their coverage and kept followers up to date through tweets in a way that today would be considered unexceptional but at the time was extraordinary. But this raised questions around professional standards, as spelling, grammar and editorial reflection went out of the window in favour of speed and instant gratification. This use of Twitter was more than just a novel method of delivery. Rather, it was about capitalising on the familiarity of the smartphone technology used every day to capture moments both personal and professional, thus helping journalists engage with their audience. But at the same time, the loss of formality that can be so valuable in the democratisation of the public sphere can also risk undermining the message that is so carefully mediated in the programme itself.

Democratisation of the news

The Arab Spring that began in late 2010 is widely recognised as a benchmark period for the power of social media to protest against dominant discourses. So much was it used as a platform for sharing dissident views and as an organisational tool for coordinating protests that the press labelled it the 'Twitter revolution' (Hill & Lashmar, 2014). And as Fiske remarked (1992: 46), "the news that people want, make and circulate among themselves may differ widely from that which the power bloc want them to have." Triggered by the self-immolation of Mohamed Bouazizi, a Tunisian street vendor whose wares had been confiscated by officials and who felt humiliated and harassed, the Tunisian revolution and wider Arab Spring saw a period of significant unrest and transition. Riots and street protests began in Tunisia to rally against the ruling parties, which led to the then-president Zine El Abidine Ben Ali stepping down and fleeing the country. The spirit of change was shared among several other North African and Middle Eastern states before the mood soured with crackdowns in Gulf states and the bloody civil wars in Syria and subsequently Yemen. The significance of the self-immolation and pictures of Bouazizi were shared throughout the world on Facebook, helping create a narrative around the man and the incident. Many of the details of this narrative remain unconfirmed or unclear. Some claimed he was a graduate (this was not true), while initial reports that he was slapped by a female official, the ultimate insult, were also found to be unsubstantiated with varying eyewitness reports. It is not fair to say that this was entirely driven by social media as mainstream news organisations also struggled with competing accounts and corrupt official voices made it difficult for reporters to find reputable sources. What is true is that social media was able to provide a voice for the voiceless and an international platform for the story to spread far more efficiently and much faster than the mainstream sources. Although there have been similar incidents in other countries before and after Bouazizi's self-immolation, they were not shared on social media in the same way and so did not raise as much awareness. Even when such an incident is covered by traditional national or local media (itself unlikely if the media are state-run or heavily censored by official powers), the impact of news is traditionally rarely felt in other countries.

Despite the potential to foster political change, social media can also be dominated by the voices of those who shout loudest, or are at least best organised in promoting their own image. This is true not least of celebrities such as Blac Chyna and Kylie Jenner who find a following on social media that exceeds that of the BBC or CNN. As Phillips observes:

> As the number of entrants rises exponentially ... only those who are most adept at using social media, most socially connected in 'real life', or already taken up by the bigger media organisations are likely to stand out.
>
> (Phillips, 2015: 90)

The invasion of a twenty-first-century private sphere such as Facebook by political or other 'hard' news can also affect the reception of the message. Newspaper readers have an expectation of bad news, shocking or upsetting news the minute they pick up a paper. They have an instinctive sense of news values (Galtung & Ruge, 1965; Harcup & O'Neill, 2001), even if they are not familiar with the theoretical frameworks. But to experience those same stories on a social media feed that is otherwise populated by family photographs, inspirational quotes or fluffy-cat pictures can heighten the impact and blurs traditional media boundaries. The image of a child in a war-torn country juxtaposed against the image of a friend's child playing happily arguably magnifies the reading of both images. Newspapers and broadcast journalists carefully consider the juxtaposition of their outputs to manage the transition from one story to the next, but this does not happen in the same way on a feed from social media platforms such as Facebook or

Twitter. Beaumont argues that today as never before the medium that carries the message shapes and defines the message itself (2011). The instantaneous nature of how social media communicate self-broadcast ideas, unlimited by publication deadlines and broadcast news slots, he continues, "explains in part the speed at which these revolutions have unravelled, their almost viral spread across a region" (ibid).

Conclusion

This chapter has discussed the ways social media platforms allow users to source their own news and to filter it to suit their politics and preferences. It provides a space for them to contribute their experiences if they are involved in stories and it is also somewhere they can give feedback to journalists. While it is clear that new platforms for broadcast journalism do provide opportunities to develop and share material with new users, it is expanding rather than fundamentally changing the processes. Traditional media sources, on whatever platform, continue to dominate and contextualise journalism that is gathered elsewhere by citizens. The process may have been opened up to the outside world, but the practice is still recognisably journalism.

Chapter bibliography

Beaumont, P. (2011) 'The truth about Twitter, Facebook and the uprisings in the Arab World', *The Guardian*, 25 February 2011. Available from: www.theguardian. com/world/2011/feb/25/twitter-facebook-uprisings-arab-libya

Bennett, S. (2012) 'Exclusive: The Twitter User Who Broke News of Whitney Houston's Death an HOUR Before the Press', *AdWeek*, 15 February 2012. Available from: www.adweek.com/digital/twitter-whitney-houston-death/

Blaine, M. (2014) *The Digital Reporter's Notebook*. London: Routledge.

Bogost, I., Ferrari, S. and Schweizer, B. (2010) *Newsgames: Journalism at Play*. Cambridge, MA: MIT Press.

Fiske, J. (1992) 'Popularity and Politics of Information' *in*: Dahlgren, P. and Sparks, C. (eds) *Journalism and Popular Culture*. London: Sage.

Galtung, J. and Ruge, M. (1965) 'The structure of foreign news: the presentation of the Congo, Cuba and Cyprus crises in four foreign newspapers', *Journal of International Peace Research*, 1.

Gillmor, D. (2006) *We The Media: Grassroots Journalism by the People, for the People*. Sebastopol, CA: O'Reilly Media Inc.

Gray, J., Bounegru, L. and Chambers, L. (2012) *The Data Journalism Handbook: How Journalists Can Use Data to Improve the News*. Sebastopol, CA: O'Reilly Media Inc.

Harcup, T. and O'Neill, D. (2001) 'What is news? Galtung and Ruge revisited', Journalism Studies, 2 (2), pp. 261–280.

Herrman, J. (2012) 'How 18-year-old Morgan Jones Told the World About the Aurora shooting', *BuzzFeed*, 20 July 2012. Available from: www.buzzfeed.com/ jwherrman/how-18-year-old-morgan-jones-told-the-world-about

Hill, S. and Lashmar, P. (2014) *Online Journalism: The Essential Guide*. London: Sage.

Hirst, M. (2011) *News 2.0 Can Journalism Save the Internet?* New South Wales: Allen and Unwin.

Jones, J. and Salter, L. (2012) *Digital Journalism*. London: Sage.

Matheson, D. and Allan, S. (2009) *Digital War Reporting*. Cambridge: Polity Press.

Pavlik, J.V. (1999) 'New media and news: implications for the future of Journalism', *New Media and Society*, 4 (1), pp. 9–27.

PEJ State of the News Media (2012) 'The role of social media in the Arab uprisings', *Pew Research Center Journalism & Media*. Available from: www.journalism.org/2012/11/28/role-social-media-arab-uprisings/#_ftn8

Phillips, A. (2015) *Journalism in Context: Practice and Theory for the Digital Age*. London: Routledge.

Rosen, J. (2006) 'The people formerly known as the audience'. Available from: http://archive.pressthink.org/2006/06/27/ppl_frmr.html

Rusbridger, A. (2009) 'The Mutualisation of News', *The Guardian*, 27 July 2009. Available from: www.theguardian.com/sustainability/report-mutualisation-citizen-journalism

Seib, P. (2002) *Going Live: Getting the News Right in a Real-Time, Online World*. Oxford: Rowman and Littlefield.

Stephens, M. (2014) *Beyond News: The Future of Journalism*. New York: Columbia University Press.

Van Dijck, T. (2009) 'Users like you? Theorizing agency in user-generated content', *Media, Culture & Society*, 31, pp. 41–58.

5   Broadcast journalism in context

Rationalising broadcast journalism

The establishment in 2006 of the Reuters Institute for the Study of Journalism at Oxford University in the United Kingdom (now located institutionally within the Department of Politics and International Relations) may well have been the point at which the study of journalism gained the ultimate recognition of its validity from the academic community. But such recognition was hard-fought over several decades and it is too early to say if more than a few skirmishes have been won in the face of some continued opposition to what is not always considered to be a 'proper' academic subject of study. This chapter takes a critical look through an academic lens at a number of aspects of broadcast journalism that share some characteristics with wider considerations of the more common field of what is often termed 'media studies'. Much of the current focus of academics working in the field has been retrained on so-called 'new' media, and in particular on social media. It is as if it were possible to 'finish' academic study of the other mass communications media, having covered every aspect possible around their production and consumption, or indeed as if it were possible for their relative maturity as communication methods to somehow disqualify them from being of any further interest academically. Sometimes it can seem as though film, newspapers, television and radio have become unfashionable in such academic circles.

Curiously, the history of media studies has traditionally followed a less than logical course in its meanderings from maverick beginnings in school classrooms where 'inoculation' of children from the perceived dangers of feature film representations began to be seen as desirable (Leavis & Thompson, 1933) to its acceptance in most countries around the world as a legitimate subject for undergraduate, postgraduate and even doctoral study. Universities such as Oxford and Cambridge had steadfastly resisted the temptation to introduce media courses or to embrace the discipline of journalism. It was only with the Reuters Institute that a first fissure opened up in one of Europe's most hallowed academic institutions. When he made his welcoming address to the Institute as chancellor of Oxford University,

Lord Patten of Barnes noted how he had often witnessed the role of journalists "making the first draft of history" and that he had needed no convincing of the importance of such work (2006). In a sense, this was hardly surprising since, throughout a distinguished political career, he had long been part of the broadcasting landscape – not least as chairman of the BBC Trust from 2011–2014. The physical location of the Institute within what was then called Green College, one of the lesser-known names in Oxford, meant it began life on the periphery. Even with its funding from the Thomson Reuters Foundation, such a conspicuous arrival at Oxford was somewhat belated after other, less apparently prestigious universities, had long included journalism within their curricula. Today the Reuters Institute has carved out a respected niche for its research, situated somewhere between the near-real-time analysis of media carried out by newspapers such as the *New York Times* and *The Guardian* and the longer-term peer-reviewed papers that can take academic journals a year or so to publish.

The history of journalism education, like that of media education in general, had also been erratic, having been removed from the national curriculum for UK schools in the 1990s and relegated to the status of a 'soft' subject for study if any time were left in the week. In the 1980s, many a schoolteacher riled in the classroom about the dominance on the UK media landscape of the Murdoch press empire, while in parallel some newspapers proclaimed their mock horror that the popular television soap opera, *EastEnders*, should be 'taught' in the classroom to unsuspecting schoolchildren, laden with left-wing propaganda as such teaching almost certainly would be (Starkey, 2017). As is often the case, the truth probably lay somewhere in the no-man's-land of the middle ground, with some excellent pedagogical practice to be found in some classrooms and the Murdoch influence on public opinion significant but not all-pervasive. Often difficult-to-engage children found dealing with important concepts around political economy, representation, audience theory, ideology and so on more palatable when using familiar case study material. Similarly, newspapers owned by News International were able to make such claims as 'It was *The Sun* wot won it' when referring to the outcome of the May 1992 general election (Street, 2001: 86). But their proprietor decided nevertheless to switch their support from the Conservative Party of Margaret Thatcher and John Major to the Labour Party of Tony Blair and Gordon Brown, when a surge of popular support for Blair and widespread contempt for the outgoing government of Major was clearly about to sweep Blair to power in a landslide victory in 1997 anyway (Starkey, 2007: 50).

Despite its difficult beginnings, media studies gained sufficient ground to become a popular A-level choice for 16–18-year-olds in UK sixth forms and colleges, as was also the case in a number of countries around the world. Usually, though, it was the practical, vocational courses in, at first, further education colleges, and then later, the growing number of 'new' or 'post-1992' universities which attracted the largest numbers of students. The UK professional accrediting bodies, the National Council for the Training of Journalists (NCTJ) and the Broadcast Journalism Training Council (BJTC) began recognising and giving their seal of approval to growing numbers of courses at vocationally-focused colleges and universities, which contributed to the exponential growth in places available for those who wanted to learn the craft of journalism. Similarly, in the less specialised field of media *production*, it was also the practical teaching, with its vaguely-hinted-at promise of a job in one or another of the media professions, which proved to be the biggest draw. As numbers of media students grew – and among them journalism students – a new breed of critic began to point out in the 1990s and 2000s that there may not be enough jobs to meet the expectations of the alleged hordes of would-be practitioners. This charge was often countered by the response that many of the skills being learned in media studies were transferable skills applicable to many different professional fields, and that group working, research, synthesising an argument, writing, presentation and other communication skills would be attractive to many employers. This response was, of course, less convincing the more specialised the skills being taught and learnt, so a highly prescriptive diet of craft skills negotiated with one of the professional bodies in journalism, such as the NCTJ or the BJTC, together with specialisms in media law, court reporting, public affairs and the use of shorthand does, however, appear much less convincingly to be a generic one.

Interestingly, as the number of media graduates employed in the media has increased, the quieter has become the once-shrill chorus of complaints from the media about the appropriateness or otherwise of media education. It is regarded much less today as the inoculation once posited by Leavis and Thompson, and others, and much more as a legitimate preparation for a vocation. The accusation that there might not be enough jobs for all those studying the media is now one much more easily levelled at a range of different disciplines, and hence less wounding to any one. There may also be a recognition that the media are indeed a collection of fast-growing industries that are also prone to rapid change and that newcomers who are able to embrace change might just be able to cut through the crowd and establish themselves in new and perhaps currently difficult-to-imagine ways. Throughout the chequered history of media education there has persisted one particular oddity: that *radio* studies should have been so slow to catch on, while early forays into film, then newspapers and television seemed to have been natural choices in schools and colleges for the more theoretically-focused media studies. In the study of media practice, too, far fewer colleges and universities in the United Kingdom offer courses in radio than in the other media, and those that do normally report much larger numbers of students applying to study the visual media than radio. Paradoxically, journalism training has tended to be polarised between print and broadcast, with the broadcast element normally being genuinely bi-media – both television *and* radio – and more recently the NCTJ broadening its scope to include broadcasting and inevitably to encroach into what was once exclusively BJTC territory.

This strategic shift reflected the steady decline in newspaper journalism already discussed, and the increasingly multimedia nature of the once exclusively print sector. It also recognises the growth of citizen journalism and its tendency to borrow broadcast reporting genres, in the making of short videos and in podcasting. The largest influence on such a transformation, though, may be the breaking down of traditional employment routes through journalism. In the 1970s, with the development of the first UK commercial radio stations, the norm was for journalists to be recruited from local newspapers, who might then have 'progressed' from radio to television. With the squeeze on paid positions in local newspaper journalism, direct entry into radio journalism has become much more common, and the latest high-definition cameras, with their hunger for fresh and essentially photogenic faces, has created a demand for suitably-endowed new recruits to enter the local and regional television industry, perhaps via a stint of weather forecasting.

Finally, in this section, what of the early ideas of Leavis and Thompson that British schoolchildren might benefit from an education that devoted some time to 'inoculating' them from the more potentially corrupting influences of Hollywood film? Chapter 1 already discussed the desirability of some form of media literacy training in order to enable citizens of democracies to play a full and effective role in their respective societies. The ideas of Leavis and Thompson, quaint as they may now seem, were perhaps no more than fledgling arguments for the more comprehensive kind of media education for which this book – and many others – have been arguing in order to counter, or at least address, the now immeasurably more complex range of voices that can be heard in the almost unbelievably more mediatised world of today. The range of academic literature on the subject is now greater than ever (De Abreu, Mihailidis, Lee, Melki & McDougall, 2017). So when media voices, such as national newspaper columnists, decry media education as either pointless or illegitimate, there is an arguably valid response which asks: just what are they trying to hide? For what purposes might media organisations or even governments want to preserve media illiteracy among their audiences, especially today in times of so-called 'fake' news, when all pioneers of media studies such as the teacher Len Masterman (1985) were advocating in individuals they taught was the development of what they called 'critical autonomy', or the ability to think sufficiently for themselves about what to trust and what not to? In order to formulate an answer to that intentionally rhetorical question, this chapter now considers what might be taught – and what might be learnt – about broadcast journalism and the ways in which that form of journalism is constructed and consumed.

Broadcast journalism in civil society

Such questions provide an opportunity to engage with some of the most important debates of our age around media and communications, while focusing and, where necessary, recontextualising them, on broadcasting in general and broadcast journalism in particular. Such academic enquiry is entirely appropriate because journalism education, like any other, should seek to pose difficult but pertinent questions about the various practices and skills being learnt in parallel with some underpinning theory: being a journalist necessarily requires an understanding of journalism, just as being a *good* journalist requires a better understanding of the contexts within which journalism takes place (Crisell, 1994) and the implications it might have on the audiences it may reach. In addressing this need, common themes include globalisation, hegemony, pluralism, trust and celebrity culture. A further question might ask what evidence there might be that broadcast journalism has been 'dumbed down', which is one of the common criticisms of not only the media, but of other walks of life, including education and politics. If such evidence exists, it might reside in the various new and emerging forms of so-called 'reality' television, namely docudrama, infotainment, celebrity culture and such 'pseudo-reality' as exemplified by television programmes like *Made in Chelsea* (E4). Such programmes purport to document the lives of real people but involve elements of coaching and performance that are simply not apparent to the viewer, and therefore make it impossible for even the most media-literate viewer to know how much is real and how much is staged for the camera and the microphone – two essential tools of the production process of which the 'cast' must, paradoxically, be very aware. In essence, the question is whether current trends in broadcasting are a precursor to the end of broadcast journalism as we know it and whether this would matter if it were the case.

Of course, discussion of some of these concepts should never be confined in a book on the study of journalism to the potential literary ghetto of a single chapter designated as 'the theory'. Many of the issues around pluralism and trust were discussed in Chapter 1 in the context of the political economy. Globalisation, too, is an issue considered in detail in Chapter 7, and inevitably, in reviewing a number of aspects of the internationalisation of the news media through online platforms, issues have been addressed around the virtual shrinking of the world into the 'global village' foreseen by McLuhan (2001). Indeed, well before that the development of satellite television began that trend, disrupting the way international agreements on the use of frequencies for terrestrial broadcasting impose on most broadcasters the requirement to operate low-power transmitters and directional antennae to avoid causing interference with the broadcasts of their near neighbours. Even more recently, the various forces of globalisation have been met with more organised resistance in a number of different countries with the growth of supernationalism. This has been evident, for example, in the United

Kingdom with the triumph in the 2016 vote to leave the European Union, in the United States with the election of Donald Trump on his 'America first' platform, and the rise of far-right parties and politicians such as Geert Wilders in the Netherlands and Marine Le Pen in France. That Wilders and Le Pen should have been defeated in national elections in their respective countries in 2017 does little to diminish the fact that behind them lay significant groundswells of nationalistic reaction among the electorates in their countries to the many and seemingly all-pervasive effects of globalisation.

In one sense, the nationalist movements had the effect of further internationalising the news agendas of their countries' national news and current affairs programming on radio and television and in the press, simply because they became the focus of attention from overseas, and therefore reaction to them from abroad became a greater part of the news agenda at home. Nonetheless, in most cases the rise of nationalism as a political force that often disrupts the traditional left-right political paradigm has been fuelled in part by the publicity that can be generated through news media, in the way that a movement may gain momentum through the publicity it generates for itself and the reactions that occur in response to it. Other forms of extremism which run counter to the homogenising effects of globalisation include terrorism and religious extremism, which can also become self-justifying and self-sustaining through being reported as part of a news agenda that contributes to the naturalisation of their existence. They can become accepted as part of the political landscape because they carve for themselves a niche in that landscape through the publicity they generate. One episode in the battle of successive governments in the United Kingdom to defeat the terrorist threat of the republican IRA saw the government of Margaret Thatcher banning the voices of members of that organisation's then political wing Sinn Féin from the airwaves of broadcast media. The ethical challenges posed by that legislation are discussed later. The episode did little to ease an already strained relationship between the broadcaster and the British government (Welch, 2005).

Hegemony, as it is commonly understood in the study of sociology and politics, means the social, cultural, ideological or economic influence exerted by a dominant group, often enduring over time and being passed down through successive generations. Some journalism can, of course, be perceived as challenging the *status quo*, in that it addresses – or even provides the oxygen of publicity to – new movements or emerging political parties. But much of it tends to provide a voice for those that already have one, to the exclusion from the public sphere of minority voices and opinions and even smaller parties which can be easily marginalised on the grounds of their already small size. Good examples of each of these approaches come from political journalism, in the way that in 2017 the broadcast media in France covered the rise of newcomer president Emmanuel Macron and his la France en Marche movement, unencumbered by the traditional party loyalties of the national newspapers, but also in the way that, over the same period in the United Kingdom, the bulk of political reporting by the broadcast media aimed to 'balance' incumbent Conservative voices against 'challenger' Labour voices. In the UK broadcast media there has long been a working concept in newsrooms and even in the narrative presented 'on air' of the 'main parties' – a label predominantly applied to the two biggest parties represented in terms of the number of seats they occupy in the House of Commons, and occasionally extended to include the traditional third party, the Liberal Democrats. The parties of the national regions, Wales, Scotland and Northern Ireland, exclude themselves from such a status because of their limited geographical coverage and therefore receive only marginal amounts of airtime in national broadcasting – although on the BBC's and ITV's regional services for those areas they are among the 'main' parties. Hence, a Plaid Cymru spokesperson would be much more likely to be included on *Wales Today* (BBC Wales) or *Wales at Six* (ITV Cymru Wales) than on either the BBC's or ITV's television news programmes and bulletins, as well as achieving much greater prominence on the independent Welsh fourth television channel's *Newyddion 9* (S4C). This phenomenon is repeated across the radio services which are either from and for Wales, and those for which Wales is but a small subsection of the total audience.

This focus on the 'main parties' may in part perpetuate those parties' continued dominance of the UK political landscape, because they are presented to the public as the limited set of possible choices at the ballot box, with any others relegated to the margins where their implied irrelevance to the final result may contribute to their marginalisation in opinion polls and, subsequently, in the eventual election results. It is difficult even for the most experienced political analysts to be entirely sure about the extent to which this hegemony of the mainstream creates a self-fulfilling prophesy and for minority parties, such as the Green Party, a vicious circle of paucity of publicity leading to underrepresentation and further marginalisation at the next and subsequent elections. A clear exception in recent years would, of course, be that of the UK Independence Party (UKIP), with its camera- and microphone-friendly former leader Nigel Farage, which gained sufficient publicity in the UK media to 'win' the 2014 European elections by receiving the most votes of all the parties contesting that election. It was perceived as posing such a threat to the Conservative Party that its then leader, David Cameron, made the offer of a referendum on the UK's continued membership of the European Union a manifesto commitment in the 2015 general election. Following the subsequent Brexit vote, UKIP's continued high profile in the UK media failed to prevent the party from languishing at just 6% in the polls for much of the 2017 general election campaign.

Notwithstanding the discussion in Chapter 1 about the requirement on the broadcast media to be impartial, the intentionally strict quota-based allocation of airtime in the UK broadcast media has not always been faithfully adhered to in practice. Close monitoring of *Today* (BBC Radio 4) during the 1997 general election revealed a very significant predominance of

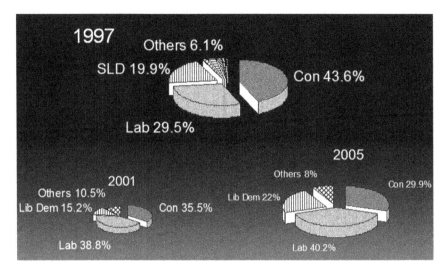

Figure 5.1 Share of airtime given to party representatives during election periods on *Today* (BBC Radio 4) in 1998, 2001 and 2005
Source: Starkey (2007).

Conservative Party voices and their access to airtime on the programme, just as the Conservatives were about to lose the election to the incoming Labour government of Tony Blair. The inherent unfairness of this favouring of the incumbent party in power, in the granting of them greater access to the microphone, was further compounded by the allocation of a more inter-ruptive interviewer, John Humphrys, to Blair than to the other two 'main party' leaders in the so-called 'set piece' party leader interviews featured on the programme in peak time in the last few days before that election. Interestingly, once Labour was in government, during the subsequent elec-tion campaigns the airtime bias was not repeated in 2001, but inverted in 2005, then with the favouring of Labour voices on the programme, as can be seen in Figure 5.1 (Starkey, 2007: 139–152).

That's entertainment

To what extent was UKIP's fall in the polls in 2017 due to a perceived redun-dancy because in its supporters' minds it had achieved its purpose and inde-pendence from Europe was by then almost certain? Alternatively, was it a consequence of the party's leadership change – not entirely seamlessly – to the arguably less charismatic Paul Nuttall in the months before the election that robbed it of the appeal of Nigel Farage? Farage's ready, personable wit and carefully cultivated 'bloke with a pint' image, together with his argu-ably more photogenic appearance, lent him some of the 'love them or loathe them' dynamic common to many celebrities – and it is largely on celebrity culture that much journalism in both broadcasting and the press now feeds in order to sustain audiences and circulation.

Undoubtedly, the camera has its favourites – people who just look better than others, even in unguarded moments. Some people are also fortunate enough to have more 'radiogenic' voices than others, which may well add to their appeal 'on air'. Shortly after his departure from the leadership of UKIP, Farage secured a regular slot on LBC, presenting a weekly political phone-in programme. Being photogenic or even radiogenic can enable personalities from politicians to pop stars, from publicists to performers and even from entrepreneurs to inventors to develop an on-air celebrity which not only enables them to promote whatever cause is dear to them, but also tends to sustain itself by perpetuating their attractiveness to audiences and producers alike – almost guaranteeing their next appearance on camera or before the microphone.

This 'stardom' can also extend beyond the charismatic types, from Nigel Farage to entrepreneurs Richard Branson and Alan Sugar, including the affable eccentrics such as the UK Foreign Secretary, Boris Johnson, and not forgetting the smooth politicians from Tony Blair to Emmanuel Macron. It also explains why broadcast journalists often maintain a roster of preferred 'talent' as ready sources, prominent in their contacts books or whatever modern electronic equivalent they prefer, and just a phone call away whenever a story breaks and a live interview or a soundbite is needed to illustrate a story or provide a counterbalancing argument to someone suddenly propelled into the limelight of a breaking news event. It touches, too, the practitioners, which is why some broadcast journalists are more likely than others to be promoted to the prestigious role of news anchor on television or high-profile presenter on an extended radio news programme. Television journalists who have found fame either through the quality of their reporting, their good looks or their charisma – or perhaps all three – include the award-winning documentary producer John Pilger, the BBC commentator and anchorman Richard Dimbleby, ITV's political editor Robert Peston, the Nixon inquisitor and satirist David Frost, the original presenter of *Question Time* (BBC1) Robin Day and – stretching the definition of 'journalist' as far as possible – the intrusive interviewers Louis Theroux and Ruby Wax.

Some of the biggest stars of television journalism are its news anchors from past and present, from Walter Cronkite (CBS) to Tom Brokaw (NBC), Huw Edwards (BBC), Trevor McDonald (ITV), Patrick Poivre d'Arvor (TF1) and Jon Snow (Channel 4). Sometimes their celebrity derives from what may in academic circles be termed 'non-diegetic events', such as the former BBC newsreader Angela Rippon participating in a sketch on the *Morecambe and Wise Show* (BBC1), in which she got up from the newsreader's desk to reveal a ballgown and began ballroom dancing with the eponymous comedians. As she was the first female national in-vision news anchor on the BBC, there are issues around gender representation that could be explored in connection with this out-of-context portrayal which inevitably involved her revealing her legs to the camera. The diegetic event which propelled Kirsty Young to instant fame on the UK's new Channel 5 in 1997, despite its disappointingly low audience figures, was the then groundbreaking practice of the newsreader standing up and even sitting *on* a desk, rather than being positioned behind it. Popular daytime news anchor Kay Burley (Sky News) is also shown moving around the studio, rather than partly concealed behind studio paraphernalia, as is far more common among her contemporaries on Sky and a number of other rolling news channels.

Dumber and dumber?

Such blurring of the often rather imprecise boundaries between journalism and entertainment – a form of spiced-up broadcast journalism with a sprinkling of celebrity – raises legitimate questions over the possibility of its being dumbed down in order to increase ratings. It is clear that in many larger broadcasting organisations, content is shared across broadcast platforms, exploiting both synergies and distinctiveness between them by using the same or similar material more than once and therefore achieving greater reach and impact. One organisation spread across more than one platform can also exploit cross-promotion, to drive audiences for one towards another, thus benefiting the brand and the organisation overall. The relatively recent trend (permitted in the United Kingdom by the regulator, Ofcom, but found elsewhere internationally) to reduce the overall duration and therefore the *scope* of the commercial radio news bulletin, together with such practices as news-hubbing, may simply be symptomatic of an overly zealous approach to the profit motive. It is certainly one which would have met with regulatory disapproval when independent radio was first launched in the United Kingdom as a concession to the commercial radio lobby, with the promise that it would offer a substantial public service in return for its incursion into ground which was traditionally the monopoly of the BBC.

It is valid, however, to ask whether this is necessarily a bad thing. Chapter 1 already noted how in many ways entertainment broadcasting brings news journalism to audiences which would otherwise not seek it out. And if a music radio station builds a larger audience through reducing speech to a minimum but retains brief hourly news bulletins, perhaps those bulletins have greater impact than if they were longer. This would seem to be a matter of compromise, in terms of finding an optimal bulletin duration that is long enough to convey the essence of a number of current news stories, while not being so long as to deter large numbers of listeners from staying tuned. In the United Kingdom, the commercial radio sector certainly seems to have come to a collective conclusion that any more than a minute or so of news on the hour is more than enough. Research for this book found ninety, or even sixty, seconds to be the practice during breakfast and day times on many stations, with stations in a few smaller groups running bulletins of up to three minutes. Such short bulletins preclude the use of location reporting, interview clips and actuality to illustrate a story, or indeed any kind of in-depth coverage of an issue, unless, of course, the editor carefully constructs a more rounded version of events over a number of hourly bulletins, building up a more accurate picture for listeners who listen over an extended period. Stories are otherwise reduced to little more than headlines, and, without live or recorded on-location reporting, the practice has removed much of the need for specialist local government reporters and for reporters skilled in court reporting *for radio*. Consequently, the radio package (Starkey, 2013) has all but disappeared from most UK commercial radio stations. It had once been a staple part of the news output of the original ILR network, and the original international and national news provider used to make available what it called 'billboards'[1] for use by stations in their own 'mixed' bulletins of international, national and local news.

Beyond the relatively simple news bulletin or extended daily news round-up, some of the larger and more ambitious ILR stations would produce documentaries and offer them to other stations in the network for broadcast free of charge, through the ILR Programme Sharing Scheme (1983–1990). A searchable archive of such recordings was developed by Bournemouth University and the British Library, and it is now curated by The British Universities Film & Video Council (BUFVC). Routine documentary pro-duction has all but disappeared from UK commercial radio even though there have been larger, national stations on air since 1992 with the arrival of Classic FM (now owned by Global). A single consolation in this sorry his-tory of radio journalism is that the digital revolution has enabled the launch of a number of national commercial speech stations in the UK, despite the often higher cost of producing original speech rather than simply playing commercially-available recorded music. London's LBC is split into two ser-vices, one on AM and the other on FM in the capital, but the FM service is broadcast nationally on DAB, and making more impact on other news media than ever before. In 2016, the Wireless Group created talkRADIO and talkSPORT2 to complement its national AM service, TalkSPORT, and all three remain on DAB and the group is now owned by Rupert Murdoch's News Corp. A further new talk station focused on business news, Share Radio, but abandoned its DAB transmission the following year to become an Internet-only service.

Despite such innovations as talkRADIO, in the United Kingdom it is now only the BBC that can be relied upon to produce a regular diet of radio doc-umentary production. But it does this with a reassuring regularity in such high-profile positions in its schedules that it seems unlikely that the radio documentary could be under threat, unless future Charter negotiations or funding settlements with the government of the day should dramatically threaten its financial resources. Radio documentary can be found not only on the Corporation's speech services, Radio 4 and Radio 5 Live, and the net-work of BBC local radio stations, but also on the 'cultural' network Radio 3

Table 5.1 Audience reach and share data for the UK's
most popular radio stations

Weekly	Reach (1,000s)	Share (%)
BBC Radio 2	15,020	18.1
BBC Radio 4	11,113	12.5
BBC Radio 1	9,103	5.6
Heart	8,715	6,3
Capital	7,761	4.1
BBC Radio 5 Live	5,341	3.6
Classic FM	5,363	3.4
Smooth	4,891	3.3

Source: RAJAR 2017.

and even on the music stations, Radios 1 and 2 – the first of which is clearly targeted at 18–25-year-olds. With the exception of the BBC's all-speech stations, Radio 4, Radio 5 Live and the World Service, the rest all balance speech and music to some degree, in a quite different, more public-service model of the compromise that has led the commercial sector to set the balance between the two much more firmly in favour of music. Interestingly, audience ratings tend to suggest that the lack of confidence in speech radio displayed by the commercial sector may be misplaced, and the only real advantage for that sector in relying so heavily on music for its music-radio output lies in the cost savings it makes through keeping speech to a minimum. The United Kingdom's most popular radio station is consistently BBC Radio 2, a station which runs extended news bulletins in daytime and through the night, conducts extended live and recorded interviews during popular peak-time sequence programmes and schedules documentaries in the evenings. Radio 1, despite the oft-repeated mantra that young people have short attention spans, also runs extended news bulletins in peak times, interviews and documentaries, and still achieves large audiences despite the very narrow focus of its youth-oriented music policy. Table 5.1 suggests the case to be derived from the audience reach and share data for the UK's most popular radio stations may be less compellingly weighted against higher speech-to-music ratios than the commercial radio sector thinks.

You're on! And *you're* not!

Does 'gatekeeping', one of the essential underpinnings of journalism theory, still have relevance in this globally connected social media environment? The term applies quite sensibly to the routine processes of selection that contribute to every kind of journalism, whatever the medium, whatever the industrial context. It quite accurately uses the metaphor of the gatekeeper who controls access to a place of privilege to which not everyone may have entry – or at least not right now. In the case of broadcasting, the place of privilege is the airtime on television or radio services, with its likely associated web presence. It is quite possible that someone, or some organisation, or even some idea that is denied access to the special place now might well be welcomed through the gate on another occasion, in the event that circumstances should differ later. Access, though, to the media can be of extreme value to a politician, a political party, a private company, one side in a dispute or any individual or organisation, especially if those people or bodies with opposing views or competing messages to promote are deprived of access or their access is more restricted. Sometimes even adverse publicity can be helpful in terms of raising awareness, but in response to adverse publicity most public relations professionals would quite sensibly seek to be allowed a right of reply. In the case of a regulated broadcasting environment, granting equal access, if the law permits it, to two or more sides in a controversy is one of the key indicators that the journalism involved is at least attempting to be impartial. Furthermore, the Ofcom regulations (2016) require gatekeeping to be broadly fair to all sides, and in the event of a successful complaint against a licensed broadcaster in the United Kingdom, tougher sanctions would almost certainly be imposed on the licensee if a response had not been sought from someone unfairly identified 'on air' as being involved in wrongdoing.

There are often statutory exceptions to the principle of fair access, too. For example, incitement to racial hatred is an offence under UK law. Although its provisions are rarely used, it would be illegal to 'balance' the views of someone who is against racism with those of someone who is outwardly racist. Including the words of the latter could be illegal if a court decided they constituted incitement to racial hatred under the Public Order Act 1986. While incitement to racial hatred has long been outlawed in the United Kingdom, that same legislation introduced the offence of incitement to religious hatred, so reporters, presenters and producers alike need to be particularly careful in live on-air situations with known or suspected racists or religious bigots, because they would be equally liable under the law if the interviewee or caller were to use a form of words that might be deemed by a court to be incitement. This book has deliberately not explored in depth other issues of libel law and intellectual property or copyright law because most of them are generic to all journalism and normally dealt with in detail elsewhere. However, because the penalties for infringing the law in any of these areas can be hard – financially and even in some cases in terms of imprisonment – every reporter, presenter or producer working in broadcast journalism needs to be a watchful gatekeeper against any person and any use of language that could impact adversely on their career. In the event of a serious indiscretion in front of a live microphone, acceptable fire-fighting practice is for the broadcaster to interrupt that person, cut that microphone and apologise, clearly disassociating the station or channel from the comments made, and making clear the nature of the problem. There are ethical issues, too, around the activities of a gatekeeper in broadcast journalism, and although ethics are discussed in more detail in the next chapter, it is worth noting here that misrepresenting an issue by inclusion can be as unethical as not 'balancing' another. An example might be giving equal weight to a maverick point of view that cruelty to animals is acceptable, that perhaps it really is acceptable to pollute the environment or, as the British anti-European Union campaigner, Nigel Farage, told a reporter, that "the doctors may have got it wrong on smoking" (Warner, 2016). Such misrepresentations would indeed constitute a form of 'fake' news.

There are various models used in journalism studies to explain the processes and outcomes of gatekeeping, but the most popular in some traditions may well be that of Galtung & Ruge (1965). By studying newsroom behaviour and the output of four newspapers, two researchers, Johan Galtung and Marie Holmboe Ruge, developed a model – or a comprehensive explanation – of what kinds of stories, or elements within stories, made them more likely to succeed in passing through the barriers of selective gatekeeping. To this essentially print-bound analysis it is important to add the aesthetics of television and radio – because someone or something that looks and perhaps also sounds attractive or striking in some way does inevitably appear more attractive to a gatekeeper in broadcast journalism. This can be most strikingly apparent as news breaks on a rolling news television channel, often because there is not much to show in the early reporting of disaster. For example, the footage of the 9/11, or September 2001, attacks on the twin towers in New York showing a plane flying into the second tower to be hit, was understandably repeated many times while commentators and reporters attempted to make sense of and provide a more detailed narrative to the events of the day.

Broadly, Galtung and Ruge identified three clusters of phenomena, namely impact, audience identification and the pragmatics of media coverage. The latter cluster is particularly pertinent in the case of television because, as Crisell observed (2004), the medium is hungry for images, preferably moving, and editorial decision-making is often dictated by that hunger. It can ultimately mean that some stories may not be covered because images are not available. That issue aside, in terms of which stories do get through the 'gate', news values in broadcast journalism still reflect remarkably closely those observed by Galtung and Ruge. New models and theories have been developed over time, as reviewed in more detail than is possible here by Allan (2004: 57–58), and among them has appeared a more recent theory of gate-*watching* by, predominantly, online news sources and users (Bruns, 2005). Gate-watching, though, presupposes that control has moved from the traditional journalistic environment to one which is a *community* of users as well as providers, 'citizen journalists' and others, and that the circulation of news is transactional rather than edited centrally – and clearly broadcast journalism, which is dominated by its broadcast element, is not there yet. As most broadcasting organisations exist using financial models which sustain them through either advertising or a licence fee, the question of how to monetise a contribution to a freely flowing, transactional model of online journalism is likely to cause reluctance until it is resolved. Like the press, broadcasting has considerable capital tied up in its traditional means of communicating with its audiences, and has therefore a vested interest in preserving those traditional models as long as possible.

Having discussed such matters as dancing anchors and squatting on desks, dumbing down and gatekeeping, as well as some of the issues raised for broadcast journalists by hegemony and politics, the next chapter explores the ethics of broadcast journalism. Those ethical standards are still firmly embedded in the normative values and professional ideas of broadcast journalists. But the combination of the competitive pressures for instant coverage of breaking news stories, cost-cutting and the pervasive nature of user-generated content is posing an unprecedented challenge to today's industry.

Note

1 'Billboard' was merely a proprietary name for 'package'.

Chapter bibliography

Allan, S. (2004) *News Culture*. Maidenhead: Open University Press.
Bruns, A. (2005) *Gatewatching: Collaborative Online News Production*. Oxford: Peter Lang.
Crisell, A. (1994) *Understanding Radio*. London: Routledge.
Crisell, A. (2004) 'Look with Thine Ears: BBC Radio 4 and Its Significance in a Multi-Media Age' *in*: Crisell, A. (ed.) *More Than a Music Box: Radio Cultures and Communities in a Multi-Media World*. Oxford: Berghahn.
De Abreu, B., Mihailidis, P., Lee, A., Melki, J. and McDougall, J. (2017) *International Handbook of Media Literacy Education*. London: Routledge.
Galtung, J. and Ruge, M. (1965) 'The structure of foreign news: the presentation of the Congo, Cuba and Cyprus crises in four foreign newspapers', *Journal of International Peace Research*, 1.
Habermas, J. (1989) *The Structural Transformation of the Public Sphere*. Cambridge: Polity.
Leavis, F.R. and Thompson, D. (1933) *Culture and Environment: The Training of Critical Awareness*. London: Chatto & Windus.
Masterman, L. (1985) *Teaching the Media*. London: Comedia.
McLuhan, M. (2001) *Understanding Media: the Extensions of Man*. London: Routledge (first published 1964).
McNair, B. (1998) *The Sociology of Journalism*. London: Arnold.
Ofcom (2016) The Ofcom Broadcasting Code. London: Office of Communications. Available from: www.ofcom.org.uk/tv-radio-and-on-demand/broadcast-codes/broadcast-code (accessed 1/3/17).
Patten, C. (2006) Opening address by The Rt Hon Lord Patten of Barnes, Chancellor of the University of Oxford, cited in 'Connecting academic research to industry challenges'. Oxford: Reuters Institute for the Study of Journalism. Available from: http://reutersinstitute.politics.ox.ac.uk/page/connecting-academic-research-industry-challenges (accessed 14/5/17).

RAJAR (2017) *Quarterly Listening, January-March 2017*. London: Radio Joint Audience Research Limited. Available from: www.rajar.co.uk/listening/quarterly_ listening.php (accessed 22/5/17).

Starkey, G. (2007) *Balance and Bias in Journalism: Regulation, Representation and Democracy*. London: Palgrave Macmillan.

Starkey, G. (2013) *Radio in Context* (2nd edn). London: Palgrave Macmillan.

Starkey, G. (2017) 'How Cinderella came late to the ball: The development of radio studies in the United Kingdom and Europe', *Central European Journal of Communication*, 1.

Street, J. (2001) *Mass Media, Politics and Democracy*. Basingstoke: Palgrave.

Warner, J. (2016) 'It's easy to mock "experts" and "the establishment". But stable government requires elites'. London: *The Telegraph*. Available from: www.telegraph. co.uk/business/2016/06/16/its-easy-to-mock-experts-and-the-establishment-but-stable-govern/ (accessed 21/5/17).

Welch, F. (2005) 'The "broadcast ban" on Sinn Fein'. London: British Broadcasting Corporation, 5 April 2005. Available from: http://news.bbc.co.uk/1/hi/4409447.stm (accessed 17/5/17).

6   The ethics of broadcast journalism

Introduction

President Trump may have lambasted CNN as a purveyor of 'fake news' in a heated and memorable press conference shortly after his election, but there is no disputing the impact of saturation coverage of the US election – ratings and advertising revenues for CNN, Fox, MSNBC and other US broadcasters soared. But were American broadcasters, seduced by the lure of financial salvation, complicit in Trump's election victory by playing to the ratings and covering his campaign more than that of rival Hillary Clinton? And what does that say about the 'Chinese wall' that has traditionally been seen as separating the news from the business of news?

This chapter explores a series of ethical issues now confronting mainstream Western news broadcasters, with a primary focus on the United Kingdom and United States. It is tempting to see an ever-growing catalogue of ethical dilemmas ushered in by the heady mix of wholesale disruption to the media business model, rampant social media and political populism. Do the boundaries between news and business, so graphically described by the metaphor of the Chinese wall, still exist or have they irreparably broken down? Have traditional values of objectivity, impartiality and fairness, epitomised by public-service broadcasting, given way to sensationalism? Is the hallowed 'right to know' being abused by intrusion and salacious gossip? And is the rush to air undermining the foundations of fact-based journalism and, as a consequence, harming public trust in broadcast news? This chapter will argue that these are in fact age-old dilemmas that go to the heart of the role of journalism in society. What is different is the speed and scale of change in today's media industry. Ethical decisions that directors of news could once ponder over a period of hours or even days now need to be addressed within minutes. When in 1988 the Conservative government of Margaret Thatcher imposed a ban on the broadcasting of the voices of Sinn Féin and several Irish Republican and Loyalist groups, the BBC and other broadcasters, outraged as they were, first trod cautiously. The ruling Conservative Party's relations with the BBC had sunk to new lows over coverage of the Northern Ireland 'troubles' and Thatcher famously expressed her opinion that "publicity is the oxygen of terrorism". Broadcasters were keen to circumvent the ban but first tried subtitling interviews with organisations subject to the ban before drawing up a list of actors who were able to voice the original words (thus pointedly making a mockery of the law and leading to its demise in 1994). Such a drawn-out process is inconceivable in today's social media environment in which the use of Twitter routinely disintermediates or bypasses mainstream news broadcasters and where competition to broadcast exclusive and engaging user-generated content is shaping the news agenda. The television producers who had to decide whether to air user-generated video material of the drummer Rigby killing in 2013 had minutes in which to weigh the ethical pros and cons of their move before committing the material to a live news bulletin.

This chapter begins by reviewing briefly the foundations of ethics in the area of broadcast news journalism, the regulatory framework and the complex relationship with other forms of media. It then explores through a series of case studies – including that of drummer Rigby – three main areas in which broadcasters are today facing recurring ethical and moral challenges. Firstly, it examines the tension between news and the business of news; secondly, it examines the benefits and risks around user-generated content, key to engaging disaffected audiences but often laden with propaganda and – all too often in the Middle East conflict – gruesome images of victims of war and terror; and finally it looks at the tension between the public's 'right to know' and the rights of individuals to privacy and protection from media intrusion.

Ethics at a time of disruption

As market forces disrupt and revolutionise media structures and practices globally, debates about ethics take on a new salience for journalists (Phillips, 2015: 126). To the excesses of the British tabloid newspaper industry, which culminated in the Leveson inquiry[1] and the closure of the scandal-tainted *News of the World*, can be added the untamed and unregulated space occupied by social media channels, citizen journalists, purveyors of fake news and Internet trolls.

The word *ethics* itself derives from the Greek *ethikos*. This can be variously translated but is generally cited as meaning 'of or for morals' (Frost, 2016: 9), thus implying moral decision-making. In the context of news, this sometimes operates at the level of a media organisation but can often come down to the everyday decisions individual journalists make, on what to cover, how to frame a story and whom they interview. As Phillips observes, journalists take on the role of moral arbiter every time they decide to reveal the sins of others and hold them up to public scrutiny – they thus have the power to do enormous harm as well as enormous good and with that power comes the need for ethical judgment (2015: 124). For many journalists, upholding on an individual basis an ethical stance is a professional badge of honour, supported by a value system often deeply ingrained within the culture of a news organisation. At the same time, however, it is recognised that news outlets have an increasing ability to spread and amplify their message, that journalists operate under intense competitive pressures and that media owners often pursue partisan interests it can be difficult to ignore. It is this tension that lies at the heart of many ethical dilemmas in journalism. It poses a simple question: is a 'good' journalist one with high principles, or one who brings his employer, within deadline, stories that will boost circulation (Frost, 2016: 11)? This tension in turn prompts society in many countries to set limits to journalistic behaviour, regulating through law (e.g. libel laws, privacy legislation, data protection) or through acceptance of voluntary codes of practice (e.g. in the United Kingdom, for many newspapers, IPSO, the Independent Press Standards Organisation).

The BBC is a classic example of an organisation in which both aspects are in play. BBC journalists and the organisation itself have a deeply embedded value system rooted in the ethos of public-service broadcasting. At the same time the BBC is now subject to official oversight by Ofcom, the independent regulator and competition authority for the UK communications industries.[2] The BBC values go to the heart of the Reithian principles of public-service broadcasting established in the 1920s and include truth and accuracy, impartiality, public interest and independence. Broadcasting was from the outset thus defined as something that was too serious to be left to the marketplace, in stark contrast to the United States where development followed an uninhibitedly commercial path (McNair, 2009: 109). The BBC's Director of News James Harding is passionate about upholding those values today, both from a corporate and individual perspective. They are, he says, non-negotiable:

> Our journalism is rooted in a set of values, an uncompromising commitment to accuracy, impartiality, to diversity of opinion and to the fair treatment of people in the news.[3]
>
> (James Harding, 2014)

For Harding, it is crucial that BBC journalists understand the impact of its journalism not only on audiences but also on the people they are reporting about. Reflecting Phillips's argument, Harding recognises what he calls the "extraordinary responsibility" as a broadcaster which, in turn, is critical if the BBC is to be respected and trusted. So long as the BBC is funded largely by the public through the licence fee, it can arguably afford to take such a high moral view of its journalism. That is not to say it can ignore competition with its commercial rivals, ITV, Channel 4 and Channel 5[4] but it has the luxury of not being reliant on advertising revenues. Generally speaking, however, the British public-service broadcasters enjoy a far greater level of trust than newspapers do. The annual trust survey for 2016 by the public relations firm Edelman (2016) showed that the BBC, ITV and Sky News all enjoyed high levels of trust by their users but many other news brands received far lower scores. In its 2016 review of British public-service broadcasting, the regulator Ofcom also concluded that the channels produced trustworthy news programmes that helped the public understand what is going on in the world (2016). However, it also noted a steady decline in the number of young people watching mainstream news programmes on television, with six in ten 16–24-year-olds using the Internet or apps for news.

Although the United States was arguably the first industrialised nation to develop an ethical code of conduct for journalists,[5] its broadcast news industry has become known over the past three decades for its highly partisan and polarised news channels, from the politically charged opposites of Fox and MSNBC to the 'shock jocks' of radio and late-night television chat shows. This partisan approach to broadcast news can be traced back to the lack of UK-style regulation and the abolition in 1987 of the so-called 'Fairness Doctrine', which had required the holders of broadcasting licences to handle matters of public interest in a way that took account of opposing sides of an argument.[6] Today Fox News' trademark slogan to be "fair and balanced" reflects a determination to counter the perceived liberal bias of broadcasters such as CNN and, as Maras observes, Fox has no qualms about addressing its audience in explicitly partisan terms (2013: 179). As such, it turns the clock back in terms of ethics to the first half of the nineteenth century before US newspapers of the day developed professional codes based on the concept of objectivity and its component parts such as fairness, impartiality and freedom from bias. According to the polling company Rasmussen Reports, Fox can boast a greater share of the 24-hour news market than its rivals. By throwing down the gauntlet to traditional rivals, it has brought into question many of the normative values of broadcast news.

The lure of ratings

The boundary or Chinese wall between news and the business of news is one of the foremost markers of the profession of journalism – not least in the United States – and reinforced through textbooks, journalism schools and in the practice of newsrooms (Coddington, 2015: 67). It is manifested in journalists' tough rhetoric against the interference of business and in a physical separation between editorial operations and advertising sales or management, often located deliberately in different parts of a media company's building. The figure of the editor often stands in the middle as a buffer, both tasked with upholding news values of independence while at the same time often being part of a news operation's management team. At times, breaches of the boundary have caused uproar, as, for example, in 1999 when it came to light that the *Los Angeles Times* had entered into a revenue-sharing deal with the Staples Center as part of a 168-page supplement about the opening of the sports arena. More than 300 *LA Times* reporters signed a petition demanding that the publisher apologise and initiate a review into any other potential conflicts of interest. But in a sense, newsrooms have always been dependent on the success of the business. And over the past decade the relentless cost-cutting and loss of journalists' jobs in both the United States and United Kingdom have exposed in a far more dramatic fashion the links between news and the finances of news as social media undermines traditional business models. In addition, a growing number of news organisations are now actively using increasingly sophisticated audience metrics and algorithms to influence the type of news they cover. On the one hand, this can be seen as a way of expanding engagement with audiences and winning back disaffected viewers or readers by tailoring news more to their needs. For Al Jazeera's Juliana Ruhfus, one of the channel's senior investigative journalists, editorial cutbacks have made journalists think more seriously about how to engage audiences and not to take them for granted. She says:

> Being a journalist no longer involves just returning to the newsroom with a version of the story on video, print and photos. Today we cater for a whole range of social media-driven platforms that engage different segments of our total audience.
>
> (Ruhfus, 2017)

But on the other hand, the extensive use of modern-day analytics also represents a clear intrusion of business into editorial decision-making that goes far beyond traditional audience surveys of the past. As the Reuters Institute for the Study of Journalism observed in a 2016 study into newsroom analytics (2016), the use is normally aligned to the business model of the given news organisation. Editorial and commercial/managerial expertise are becoming intertwined in today's digital environment.

As these examples illustrate, challenges to the Chinese wall tend to come at times when news organisations are facing financial pressures, and nowhere has the challenge been more graphically illustrated than in the 2016 US election campaign. A 24-hour news channel such as CNN, which shot to prominence with its live coverage of the 1991 Gulf War out of Baghdad, has been dependent on fees paid by cable providers to include it in its package of channel offerings. The public would tune in to CNN for live breaking news, typically a natural disaster or school shooting. But breaking news on that scale does not happen every day, and the rise of social media in recent years meant fewer consumers were willing to pay for cable packages. Then along came the Trump election campaign, his anti-establishment rhetoric and raucous campaign rallies. As the *New York Times* put it in a post-election analysis of the channel: "*CNN had a problem, Trump solved it.*" The newspaper concluded:

> Had Trump lost the election, CNN would probably have returned to its previously scheduled struggle for survival. Instead, it has become more

central to the national conversation than at any point in the network's history since the first Gulf War.

(Mahler, 2017)

CNN, together with other news networks, provided saturation coverage of Trump's campaign. According to an analysis of the 2016 election by the Shorenstein Center on Media, Politics and Public Policy, Trump received 15% more press coverage than his presidential rival Hillary Clinton.[7] The Center concluded that the secret to Trump's wider coverage lay in the controversial nature of the story he offered:

> Trump's dominant presence in the news stemmed from the fact that his words and actions were ideally suited to journalists' story needs. The news is not about what's ordinary or expected. It's about what's new and different, better yet when laced with conflict and outrage. Trump delivered that type of material by the cartload.
>
> (Patterson, 2016)

The focus among the US media outlets monitored was almost exclusively on the 'horse race' and the controversies surrounding the two main candidates, with actual policy issues taking up only 10% of the news coverage. Although Trump dominated coverage, it was overwhelmingly negative against him. The Shorenstein Center found that Fox News was the most favourable, but even in this case negative stories outweighed positive ones by a ratio of three-to-one.

For the American news industry, and particularly broadcasters such as CNN and Fox, the campaign was akin to pulling in Super Bowl advertising revenues for several weeks on end. As the *New York Times* put it, Trump provided drama and conflict every time he opened his mouth (Mahler, 2017). "Indeed," it said, "it often seemed disconcertingly as though Trump had built his entire campaign around nothing so much as his singular ability to fill cable news's endless demand for engaging content." The US media analytics company mediaQuant calculated that Trump received the equivalent of $5.0 billion in free media or 'earned media' compared with Clinton's $3.2 billion. And while ratings fell back after the election, Fox News, in number one position, was still showing a 35% gain in viewers in January 2017 compared to a year earlier. According to the analytics company Nielsen Research, in the first three months of 2017 Fox enjoyed the best quarter in the history of 24-hour cable news. CNN was off its election campaign peak ratings but the first quarter of 2017 was still its best for 15 years. Of course, journalism needs to be financially sound to flourish and to be able to carry out its core mission of upholding democracy and holding power to account. But critics such as the *New York Times* have highlighted the symbiotic relationship between Jeff Zucker, the president of CNN Worldwide, and Trump.

This can be traced back to the president's starring role in *The Apprentice*, the reality TV show that Zucker, then president of NBC Entertainment, first brought to American screens. Did CNN's and other networks' saturation coverage of the Trump campaign aid his rise to the presidency? Or was it simply the product of Trump's television experience and his ability to manipulate today's media to his advantage? Arguably both elements were at play, and certainly Trump's Republican critics and rivals during the primary campaigns accused CNN of giving him more airtime than they received. Zucker, for his part, has been robust in defending CNN and has argued that Trump granted the media greater access than other candidates did. The one thing that is clear is that the boundaries between news and entertainment became very porous during the US election campaign.

The British system of public-service broadcasting is specifically designed to prevent television and radio news chasing ratings in such a way, setting out a clear regulatory regime under Ofcom that requires equal airtime for political parties[8] (in stark contrast to British newspapers, which have no such qualms about taking party-political positions). That is not to say that the BBC and other broadcasters are not routinely criticised for political bias. The BBC explicitly recognises that in its guidelines to journalists, saying: "There is no area of broadcasting where the BBC's commitment to due impartiality is more closely scrutinised than in reporting election campaigns." It goes on to say:

> To achieve due impartiality, each bulletin, or series of summaries, daily programmes or programme strands, as well as online and interactive services, for each election covered, must ensure that the parties (and, where relevant, independent candidates) are covered proportionately over an appropriate period, normally across a week, or for weekly programmes across the campaign as a whole.
>
> (BBC, 2017)

The difference with US news channels could not be starker, but that is not to say that the BBC is ignoring ratings or its audience. It too is making increasing and extensive use of analytics. The Reuters Institute for the Study of Journalism highlighted in a 2016 report into media's use of analytics how the BBC has set up an 'audience development team' (not necessarily made up of journalists) with the aim of giving data and analytics a more central role in the newsroom. The aim is that journalists become familiar with dashboards and data, sharing insights in editorial meetings and fostering audience engagement. The study concludes that although journalists initially resisted the introduction of such metrics into their news culture, opinions have started to shift to curiosity and interest.

The contrasting approaches towards election coverage in the United Kingdom and United States highlight the way in which regulation of broadcasters has diverged over the recent past and the critical ethical questions that are posed by the growing financial pressures on news organisations. As Frost observes, their increasing market orientation has meant that all but the public-broadcasting sector have been more concerned with chasing audiences than presenting what many call quality news (2016: 36). The pre-occupation with metrics to quantify audience interest can end up replacing news judgment with an incomplete view of the audience which is driven by commercial considerations (Coddington, 2015: 77). Sometimes, as illustrated above, this tension goes to the heart of how broadcasters cover elections, one of the cornerstones of democracy. At other times, it manifests itself in a competitive rush to bring breaking news to the screen first, pitting the need for speed against accuracy (one of the age-old pressures faced by news agencies such as Reuters and the Associated Press) and often raising issues of public taste and decency. The next section of this chapter explores these tensions through examination of coverage of a series of high-profile terror attacks and violent conflicts that have dominated breaking news programming in the recent past.

Never wrong for long – the rush to air

The pace of technological change has taken a quantum leap forward in the past decade and introduced intense new time pressures on broadcast news journalists. It is worth reflecting first on an era not so long ago, when broadcasters had the luxury of debating the ethical pros and cons of their actions over a period of days and, sometimes, weeks.

Back in September 2004, in the wake of the second Gulf War, an Islamic extremist group *Tawhid and Jihad* kidnapped in Baghdad a 62-year-old British civil engineer Kenneth Bigley, demanding the release of Iraqi women prisoners held by the coalition forces. Within two days of the kidnapping, a video was released of Bigley and two US hostages he had been working with. The Americans were beheaded in the next days but Bigley's ordeal was to be played out over a further two-and-a-half weeks. Two further videos were released showing him caged and dressed in an orange jumpsuit reminiscent of those used at the Guantanamo Bay US detention camp. In these, he pleaded for his life directly to the then UK prime minister, Tony Blair. Despite his pleas, an international campaign for his release and an attempted escape, Bigley was beheaded in Fallujah three weeks after his capture.

The videos were posted widely on blogs but for broadcasters the footage posed a classic dilemma reminiscent of Thatcher's concern about news coverage of militant groups in the Irish conflict: should broadcasters be giving the Islamic terror group the oxygen of publicity? There was in fact no policy about beheading-videos in place at major British broadcasters. But crucially there was time in 2004 for a debate on the issue, and it actually played out in public while Bigley's fate was unknown and still in the balance. Critics said broadcasting the tapes would simply encourage more hostage-taking. Blair himself, in an interview in *The Observer* newspaper, said the hostage-takers

holding Bigley were manipulating the media in pursuit of their goal of desta-
bilising Iraq. He said they believed they could "use and manipulate the modern media to gain enormous publicity for themselves and put democratic
politics and politicians in a very difficult position". Others maintained that
the Bigley videos were news and to suppress them would be a form of censorship. The BBC's Head of Newsgathering, Adrian van Klaveren, argued
that the videos contained "real information" and that it was vital to show
them as long as proper context and explanation were provided. But as the
crisis continued, the BBC's use of footage became more restrained, and by
the time that in November of the same year the British nurse Margaret
Hassan was kidnapped in Baghdad the BBC had in fact re-evaluated its policy on the handling of videos. As a result, the BBC, Sky and ITN all became
more conservative in their broadcasting of videos of her, particularly avoid-
ing material showing her in obvious distress. Many preferred to use still
images or 'frame grabs' rather than broadcast a moving image with sound.
The BBC's Head of News at the time, Roger Mosey, said:

> What we have to do is, on a case-by-case basis, balance the news value
> against the level of personal stress and duress the person is under. I think
> what we have here is someone who appears to be in a state of acute dis-
> tress, therefore we have to ask what is the merit of playing it on national
> TV? There is no gain to see a woman in acute distress.[9]

Fast-forward just one decade, and the next generation of beheading-footage
was not delivered to newsrooms by video cassette or redistributed via Al
Jazeera but was posted online directly by web-savvy followers of ISIS, so-
called Islamic State. Starting in the middle of 2014, a series of beheading-
videos emerged through social media online, once again with many of the
Western victims clad in orange jumpsuits. British media's fascination with
the stories was heightened by the discovery that one of the ISIS militants pic-
tured wielding a knife clearly had an English accent. Dubbed 'Jihadi John',
he was subsequently revealed to be Muhammed Emwazi, of Iraqi origin,
whose family had settled in London when he was six years old. The appearance of these videos seemed to usher in a new age in which images take on
added significance. The author Will Self put it as follows:

> The ubiquity of the image in our lives, and the new ontology of imagery,
> is the stage on to which Jihadi John and the other Islamic State murder-
> ers have made their swaggering entrance … ours is the culture of the
> repeat, the freeze-frame and the slow-motion action sequence.
>
> (Self, 2014)

Of course, terrorists have always sought to place images of their victims in
the media as a propaganda tool, from the days of the Red Army Faction
(RAF) and the black-and-white pictures they sent by post to newspapers in

the 1970s (for example, that of the kidnapped German industrialist Hanns Martin Schleyer). But with hindsight these images appear to be remarkably restrained. As Linfield argues, we are now witnessing with ISIS a fundamental shift in the use of 'perpetrator images':

> We live in the age of the fascist image. The cell-phone camera and lightweight video equipment – along with YouTube, Facebook, Instagram, and all the other wonders of social media – have allowed perpetrators of atrocities to document, and celebrate, every kind of violence, no matter how grotesque.
>
> (Linfield, 2015)

The ethical dilemma posed by such footage remains the same as it was at the height of the Iraqi beheading tapes a decade earlier – whether to broadcast or not. But, crucially, the time for decision-making by news executives or producers has in the intervening decade shrunk to what is sometimes a matter of minutes. Most often, the material is already circulating on social media platforms, posing mainstream broadcasters the question of whether they should be following suit and, if so, what they should actually be showing to their audiences. As it was, UK broadcasters were careful not to show anything close to a beheading, although chilling still images of Jihadi John poised over hostages with a knife were used. This prompted criticism that he and ISIS were being glamourised by the coverage. The BBC reported that it had received "some complaints from viewers and listeners who feel there has been too much coverage" of the story.[10] But at the same time, it forcefully justified its reporting of Jihadi John's identification, arguing that it was important to understand his background and how he had become radicalised.

Harrowing footage of the victims of chemical weapons attacks on Syrian civilians have also put broadcasters on the spot. In a sense, social media has enabled almost instantaneous reporting of what are clearly major human rights violations and allowed important stories to be told. In 1988, when the Iraqi dictator Saddam Hussein had gassed his own Kurdish population at Halabja, it had taken five days for that massacre to emerge. A quarter of a century later, when a chemical weapons attack struck civilians in the Damascus suburb of Ghouta, social media was flooded almost immediately with graphic video footage of children writhing in agony. Nabila Ramdani, a French-Arab journalist who had worked extensively in Syria, recounted how her contacts in the country sent her almost contemporaneously video footage of children dying from the effects of nerve agents. And as a result, UN inspectors were swiftly sent into Syria. Equally, a sarin gas attack on the Syrian town of Khan Sheikhoun in 2017 killed at least 86 civilians, with disturbing images emerging quickly of dozens of children who had been killed or injured. In both cases, the dilemma for broadcasters was not *whether* to cover the story (and the question of who was responsible) but *what* to show. It was very quickly apparent that the Khan Sheikhoun attack would have significant ramifications on the world's political stage, including a *de facto* reversal of US policy towards the Syrian president Bashar al-Assad. As a result, there was consensus among broadcasters that the use of graphic footage of victims, however disturbing, was an essential part of telling the story. There was indeed no shortage of harrowing video of children gasping for breath, fanning international outrage. Newscasters took the precaution of warning viewers that they would be broadcasting disturbing images, and to date the British regulator Ofcom has not registered enough complaints to prompt an investigation.

Ofcom certainly did investigate viewers' complaints about UK news coverage following the 2013 killing of the off-duty soldier drummer Lee Rigby. On 22 May 2013, Rigby was hacked to death in broad daylight outside his barracks in Woolwich, London. His two assailants calmly engaged passers-by in conversation, waiting to ensure that they were captured by mobile phone footage before the arrival of the police. Video of one of the attackers wielding a machete in his bloodied hands was bought and used by the tabloid newspaper *The Sun* and on television by ITV News, prompting almost 700 complaints to Ofcom. Most major daily newspapers used 'screen grabs' from the footage for their front pages the next morning. Of course, a decade ago, that footage was unlikely to have existed since mobile phones had only just begun to incorporate the high-resolution cameras and video capability, both of which are today standard. Similarly, when Amedy Coulibaly took hostages in a Paris supermarket in the wake of the 2015 Charlie Hebdo massacre, he came armed not just with a Kalashnikov but also a GoPro[11] camera strapped to his torso. He tried (but failed) to email footage of his attack, including his killing of three shoppers, from a computer in the supermarket. These incidents are typical of how media has become deeply embedded in our everyday life, even at the level of terror. As Deuze observes, people nowadays know that everything they do in life could be recorded, archived, edited, redacted and publicised on a continuous basis – it is a world that lives in the moment of recording itself (2012: 261). It follows therefore that this footage, if considered newsworthy, is likely to find its way onto television screens and not be restricted to social media sites. In the case of the drummer Rigby footage, the producers at ITV News had little time to review the exclusive material they had bought before airing it on their 6.30pm teatime news bulletin. But after it played out, viewers called in to complain that the pictures of the bloodstained assailant had been used, half of the complainants saying it was too early in the day and could have been viewed by children. The news bulletin was indeed clearly before the so-called 9pm watershed that operates in the United Kingdom, a cut-off point before which Ofcom rules that material unsuitable for children should not generally be shown. It categorises unsuitable material as including everything from sexual content to violence, graphic or distressing imagery and swearing. But when in January 2014 Ofcom delivered its ruling, it decided that the footage had *not* breached broadcasting regulations and was justified by the context and "unprecedented nature of the incident". It did, however, issue new guidelines on the need to give warnings before airing distressing content.

But there are also numerous examples of broadcasters covering breaking terror stories where the rush to bring live footage or social media material to the screen has led to major factual mistakes being made live on air. There is indeed a sorry history of such incidents. As long ago as 1999, a witness phoned in to a US television network describing the Columbine High School massacre in Denver only for it to emerge he had been watching it unfold live on cable news miles away (in fact, in Utah) like the rest of the nation. One of the local television stations ran a school yearbook picture of one of the shooters, Eric Harris. But it turned out not to be him but a classmate instead. Despite internal memos, the false picture was repeatedly broadcast over affiliate stations. In fact, the coverage of the Columbine shooting has become a case study in the problems that can occur when the media descends en masse on the scene of such a traumatic news story. The American journalist and media commentator Alicia Shepard described how by the second day the number of satellite trucks around the school had grown from about 20 (local Denver stations) to as many as 150 as the national networks and international broadcasters descended. It was, she wrote:

> Riveting drama for daytime television. Breathless high school students in fear of their lives. Mad assassins inside a school. Nearly 2,000 high school hostages. Frantic parents. A situation out of control … no resource would be tested more than the ability to make snap decisions about what to air that first day under enormous pressure.
>
> (Shepard, 2003)

Going live at lunchtime, with scant details of what was actually happening, the dilemma was what footage to show. Some of the first accounts coming from witnesses were understandably confused, leading to the myth (since debunked) of the two killers, Harris and Dylan Klebold, being members of a group called the 'Trenchcoat Mafia'. Cameramen shot scenes of the dead and wounded, with blood and without blood, leaving it to control rooms to decide what to broadcast. When the first anniversary of the shooting came, parents of children who had been shot dead or injured pleaded with television stations not to rebroadcast footage. Few broadcasters felt they could agree to that, but the call did lead to an element of restraint. And in 2015 a national campaign called *No Notoriety* was launched in the United States, urging the media not to name or show pictures of mass killers and not to broadcast self-serving statements made by them.

The culture of pack journalism that such stories attract is little different in Europe, even in a country like Germany where public-service broadcasting is deeply entrenched. When the co-pilot Andreas Lubitz deliberately crashed Germanwings' Flight 9525 into the French Alps on 24 March 2015, all 150 people on board were killed. It didn't take long for media to discover that among the victims was a group of 16 German students, 14 girls and two boys, and two of their teachers, from Joseph-Koenig school in Haltern am See, Western Germany. The group was travelling back home from a Spanish exchange programme on the Germanwings flight and quickly became the focus of mass media attention. What followed, as German and international press descended on Haltern, a small town of 37,000 people, is similar to events in Dunblane in 1996 (when media besieged a school in Scotland after a mass shooting) and caused widespread outrage among the population. One of the students who had not been on the exchange trip, Mika Baumeister, went home at lunchtime as news of the crash was breaking and returned to the school later to find the area besieged by journalists. He set out his feelings in a blog that revealed distaste for the way media frame such stories:[12]

> By 5.30pm, when I had returned to school, the scene had started to resemble a human zoo, with the press behind their barricades ogling us students. Even though there was still not 100% confirmation of the deaths, there were already lots of tears. We felt as if the press were just waiting for our response to the final confirmation to film us, the emotionally destroyed people.

Baumeister told of the underhand tricks journalists had used to try to interview classmates of those who had died in the crash and reported that they were being offered up to 80 Euros to speak on camera:

> One journalist reportedly put on an emergency pastoral care unit waistcoat to get access to the students. It appears that others approached mourners at the candles with a tape recorder in their pockets to record conversations; a mobile phone in a bouquet of flowers was allegedly used to take exclusive pictures. One person tried to disguise himself as a teacher – at a school that is so small that the roughly 80 teachers are known to everyone. How in the world could someone even come up with such a desperate idea?

When in Munich in summer 2016 a lone gunman lured and shot dead nine young people at a McDonald's restaurant, German broadcasters switched to live footage and some of them blended in Twitter feeds. This contributed to panic in the city, with tweets suggesting that there were multiple gunmen involved in the attack, marauding in major tourist areas and recalling the 2015 ISIS terror attack on Paris. The police, also resorting to Twitter, urged the public not to publish photos or videos online, asking instead that anything be uploaded to their own site to help in the investigation. In the final analysis there was no link between the Iranian-born German attacker David Sonboly and ISIS. To their credit, German broadcasters did not make the connection and showed restraint. But that did not prevent international media speculating that this could be a case of Islamic terrorism. The confusion of live coverage of a breaking news story was also evident in the 2017 'lone-wolf' attack on Westminster when 52-year-old Briton Khalid Masood mowed down pedestrians before stabbing to death a policeman outside parliament. British television channels broadcast graphic eyewitness mobile phone video of victims lying on the ground. Broadcasters also showed video of a woman who had been hit by Masood's car being flung into the Thames. Although she was rescued from the water, she later died. As was the case in the Columbine shooting, a serious reporting error was made, with Channel 4 issuing an apology after they named the wrong man as the perpetrator.

The social media footage of the Westminster attack recalled the drummer Rigby video and encapsulated the ethical dilemmas. On the one hand, this was an ISIS-inspired attack in broad daylight on innocent citizens in the heart of London and the institution of parliament. Clearly it was a major news story of importance to the nation. On the other hand, the footage used came very close to breaching Ofcom's guidelines, the rush to air led to mistakes, and saturation coverage played into the hands of the attacker's quest for publicity. Ofcom's code on covering suffering and distress states:

> Broadcasters should not take or broadcast footage or audio of people caught up in emergencies, victims of accidents or those suffering a personal tragedy, even in a public place, where that results in an infringement of privacy, unless it is warranted or the people concerned have given consent.
>
> (Ofcom, 2013, section 8.16)

It can be argued that in this respect broadcasters did behave responsibly and were careful not to use footage that identified victims by showing their faces (or pixelated it) and the footage of the Romanian woman being thrown over the bridge parapet had been shot at a great distance. Once again, it is an age-old dilemma of whether to use images or not, with the crucial difference that the decision-making process has been reduced to just minutes by the availability of social media.

The right to know or invasion of privacy

Such attacks generated immense public interest at a time when a growing sense of unease has spread through the populations of major cities such as London, Paris and Munich. It can be argued that the use of graphic footage, within the constraints of regulation, is justified and actually needed to illustrate the significance of a breaking news story. What, then, of stories that might interest the public but not be of public interest? It is hard to deny that at times of competitive pressure the 'right to know' can sometimes be an excuse to broadcast sensationalist material aimed at boosting audience share at the expense of an individual's privacy. Archard defines privacy as keeping personal information non-public or undisclosed (2000: 83). While France and several other European countries have privacy laws or protection for individuals through their constitutions, Britain had historically had no such law until the 1998 European Rights Act, which incorporated into law the European Convention on Human Rights. Despite this, the tabloid newspapers are renowned for delving into the private lives of individuals, for their fascination with celebrities and 'stings' designed to lure big names into embarrassing situations. The 2011–2012 Leveson judicial inquiry laid bare a tawdry tale of phone-hacking, corruption and desperate levels of 'muckraking' aimed at propping up a constant decline in newspaper sales. Public trust in some sections of the media, particularly the written press, plunged to an all-time low, with the late British media commentator Steve Hewlett labelling it the worst crisis to engulf the press in modern times (2011: 23). The academic Steven Barnett speaks of "tasteless practices" of the British tabloids and the tawdry side of media (2016).

Certainly in the United Kingdom the regulatory regime around broadcasting has meant television and radio is less likely to intrude on a celebrity's privacy; although even here, as the market becomes increasingly dominant, this restraint is being eroded (Frost, 2016: 5). The BBC in its *Editorial Guidelines* (2017) asks staff to consider whether a story is in the public interest, adding that the more private or intimate the information is, the greater the public-interest justification needs to be.[13] Put another way, the age-old adage that people in the public eye or celebrities are 'fair game' is not defensible. It is far more persuasive to argue that a person's privacy can be breached if it can be shown to be in the public interest (Archard, 2000: 88). Morrison and Svennevig point out that while there are numerous examples of what is judged to be in the public interest, there is no clear definition and that judgments can change from society to society (2007: 45).

The BBC learnt how hard it is to balance these priorities and the debate around such values when the popular singer Sir Cliff Richard sued the Corporation after it had used a helicopter to broadcast live coverage of a police raid on his home in 2014. The police raid took place against the background of a series of investigations into public figures and also of historical sexual abuse. Sir Cliff was never arrested or charged and argued that the BBC had colluded with the police to gain access to the raid.

> I've never known, I don't think, investigations take place with lighting and cameras and special angles for the helicopter [he told the *Daily Telegraph* in an interview]. I feel I have every right to sue because, if nothing else, definitely for gross invasion of my privacy.

He spoke of two years of emotional trauma while he had been under investigation and argued that individuals should not be named unless charged – one of the conclusions of the Leveson report. The BBC did apologise for causing the singer distress but it defended robustly its coverage on the grounds of public interest. The BBC said in a statement:

> Once the South Yorkshire Police had confirmed the investigation and Sir Cliff Richard's identity and informed the BBC of the timing and details of the search of his property, it would neither have been editorially responsible nor in the public interest to choose not to report fully the investigation into Sir Cliff Richard because of his public profile.

Critics of the BBC, including parliamentarians and the human rights lawyer Geoffrey Robertson, argued that it had been under competitive pressure to generate exclusive footage after being behind to its main commercial rival ITV over coverage of the drummer Rigby killing. The legal case brought by Sir Cliff against the BBC is currently in the High Court.

This bitterly disputed case illustrates once again how broadcast news, even in the context of Britain's highly regulated public-service regime, is driven by competitive pressures and how the lines between what should and what should not be shown are becoming increasingly blurred and contested. Other cases seem clearer-cut and have caused public outrage as reporters have been deemed to cross an ethical line, sometimes intruding into private grief.

This was the case in 2014 after the downing of Malaysian Airlines' Flight MH17 by a missile strike over eastern Ukraine. *Sky News* journalist Colin Brazier, anchoring the broadcaster's live reporting from the scene of the wreckage, stooped down and was seen handling items among the debris, including a child's water bottle and a set of keys. Brazier immediately recognised that he had stepped over a moral line and apologised at once live on air. Ofcom received 205 complaints and Sky 59 directly. Writing later in *The Guardian*, he told how he had been overcome by emotion:

> During that lunchtime broadcast I stood above a pile of belongings, pointing to items strewn across the ground. Out of the corner of my eye I spotted a pink drinking flask. It looked familiar. My six-year-old daughter, Kitty, has one just like it.
>
> I bent down and, what my Twitter critics cannot hear – because of the sound quality of internet replays of the broadcast – is that I had lost it. It is a cardinal sin of broadcasting, in my book anyway, to start blubbing on-air. I fought for some self-control, not thinking all that clearly as I did so. Too late, I realised that I was crossing a line.
>
> (Brazier, 2014)

Ofcom said after its investigation that it had taken into account the "unusual and emotionally charged situation" Brazier found himself reporting on, but found that his actions were capable of causing considerable offence. A year later, the same charge was levelled against reporters from CNN, MSNBC and some other US networks as they swarmed into the house of suspects who had shot dead 14 people in San Bernardino, California. The reporters were seen live on air rummaging through baby gear and photographs and handling an ID. Here the offence was not just intrusion and insensitivity; the reporters were also accused of compromising a crime scene and potential evidence. MSNBC came under strong criticism for broadcasting pictures and IDs of people who were not known as suspects.

Conclusion

All the news stories discussed in this chapter share one thing in common: they have illustrated familiar ethical problems and dilemmas which have been the subject of journalistic debate ever since the emergence of the objectivity paradigm in the United States and Britain at the end of the nineteenth century. The US election demonstrated the perpetual tension between the chase for ratings and the values of impartiality and freedom from bias; the rush to be first to air with news on a spate of terrorist attacks led to a series of factual reporting errors that could have been avoided; chemical weapons attacks in the Syrian conflict posed the question as to whether distressingly graphic images should be used to illustrate the gravity of a story; and the competitive scramble to report from the scene of MH17 or from the home of the San Bernardino shooting suspects led to reporters overstepping the line and gross intrusion.

What has, however, changed beyond recognition is the broader media landscape. Competitive pressures to re-engage disaffected audiences, and in some cases for financial survival, have increased exponentially, stemming from the demise of media's traditional twentieth-century business model and from social media rivals. User-generated content has provided exciting new opportunities to see conflict and terror unfold in virtual real-time, but producers and programme directors are now having to make minute-by-minute decisions they would have previously been able to ponder for hours. And the rolling format of news means that mistakes caused by undue haste to broadcast can often be glossed over without consequence as the headlines are continuously reworked, leading to the facetious jibe that 24-hour channels are 'never wrong for long'.

Critics are starting to ask whether this new instantaneous environment is distorting broadcasters' ethical judgment and whether we should return to earlier values. *The Guardian* columnist Simon Jenkins accused the BBC of overreacting with its saturation coverage of the Westminster attack and effectively aiding and abetting terrorists by giving them the publicity and prominence they seek. The attack should, he said, be treated as a crime, much in the way that IRA bombings, which often targeted London, were treated in the past.

> All over London people are doing crazy things with knives, in cars, and people are dying [Jenkins said on the BBC's *Newsnight* programme]. This happens to have taken place in Parliament, which is indeed serious,

and people have died. I'm not underplaying it at all and it should be publicised. It's quite different from ascribing it with this tremendous clutter of politics, and Islam and religion – it's quite wrong.

(Jenkins, 2017)

His criticism echoes that of Helen Boaden, the former Director of BBC News, and her plea for "slow news" as a counterweight to the instantaneous news now dominating the media landscape.[14] For her, public-service broadcasters must adhere to their age-old values of good journalism – impartiality, accuracy, expertise and evidence – and resist being pulled in the same direction as all the others. It is, of course, not feasible to turn the clock back to an analogue age when RAF terrorists sent black-and-white pictures of their hostages to newspapers; or even to the video cassettes of al Qaeda. Nor is it possible to deny the existence of the globally connected world of instantaneous communication we now live in. But there is a strong case for all news organisations and journalists to have a sound background in ethics and moral values; and for them to have thought through in advance many of the issues that require instantaneous on-air decisions in today's era of live breaking news.

Notes

1 The former UK prime minister David Cameron announced a two-part inquiry investigating the role of the press and police in the phone-hacking scandal on 13 July 2011. The "Inquiry into the Culture, Practices and Ethics of the Press" was chaired by Lord Justice Leveson. Its 2,000-page report, published in November 2012, recommended a new body to replace the widely discredited Press Complaints Commission and was highly critical of the newspaper industry, saying some of its behaviour ranged from the criminal to the indefensibly unethical. See: http://webarchive.nationalarchives.gov.uk/20140122145147/; www.levesoninquiry.org.uk/; http://webarchive.nationalarchives.gov.uk/20140122145147/; and www.official-documents.gov.uk/document/hc1213/hc07/0780/0780.asp

2 Ofcom became the official regulator of the BBC in April 2017.

3 See BBC Academy website: www.bbc.co.uk/academy/journalism/values/article/art20130702112133786

4 With the emergence of commercial rivals to the BBC, starting with ITV's establishment in 1955, the government imposed certain public service obligations, requiring a certain level of news, arts and religious programming. Requirements were also placed on Channel 4 and Channel 5.

5 The Kansas Editorial Association's Code of Ethics for the Publisher was written in 1910 and set out a code of practice for advertising departments, circulation and news (Frost, 2016: 281).

6 Pressure to abolish the doctrine arose in the 1980s, with arguments that it was not compatible with the First Amendment of the US Constitution and rights to freedom of speech.

7 The research was based on the election coverage in the print editions of five daily papers (*Los Angeles Times*, *The New York Times*, *The Wall Street Journal*, *The Washington Post* and *USA Today*) and the main newscasts of five television networks (ABC *World News Tonight*, CBS *Evening News*, CNN *The Situation Room*, Fox *Special Report* and NBC *Nightly News*).

8 Ofcom, for example, stipulates that a party qualifies for an election broadcast if it is contesting one sixth or more of the seats up for election in a 'first past the post' system.
9 See: www.theguardian.com/media/2004/oct/22/iraqandthemedia.iraq
10 See: www.theguardian.com/media/2015/mar/05/bbc-defends-mohammed-emwazi-coverage
11 The GoPro company was founded in 2002 and specialises in small video cameras that can be 'worn' and are typically used to capture action photography and extreme sports.
12 See: http://meistergedanke.de/2015/umgang-der-medien-mit-schuelern-und-angehoerigen-in-haltern/43#comment-89; and http://meistergedanke.de/2015/cost-what-it-may-media-in-haltern/189
13 See: www.bbc.co.uk/academy/journalism/article/art20130702112133653
14 See Chapter 2.

Chapter bibliography

Archard, D. (2000) 'Privacy, the public interest and a prurient public' *in:* Kieran, M. (ed.) *Media Ethics*. London: Routledge.
Barnett, S. (2016) 'The Tragic Downfall of British Media', *Foreign Policy*, 8 July 2006. Available from: http://foreignpolicy.com/2016/07/08/the-tragic-downfall-of-british-media-tabloids-brexit/
BBC (2017) *Editorial Guidelines*. London: British Broadcasting Corporation, www.bbc.co.uk/editorialguidelines/
BBC (2017) *Election Guidelines*. London: British Broadcasting Corporation. Available from: http://downloads.bbc.co.uk/guidelines/editorialguidelines/pdfs/2017FINALElectionGuidelines3_3_17.pdf
Brazier, C. (2014) 'MH17: My error of judgement', *The Guardian*, 22 July 2014. Available from: www.theguardian.com/media/2014/jul/22/mh17-sky-news-reporter-colin-brazier-crash-victims-luggage
Coddington, M. (2015) 'The wall becomes a curtain: revisiting journalism's new-business boundary' *in:* Carlson, M. and Lewis, S. (eds) *Boundaries of Journalism: Professionalism, Practices and Participation*. London: Routledge.
Deuze, M. (2012) *Media Life*. Cambridge: Polity.
Edelman Trust Barometer (2016) Available from: www.edelman.com/insights/intellectual-property/2016-edelman-trust-barometer/
Frost, C. (2016) *Journalism Ethics and Regulation*. Abingdon: Routledge.
Harding, J. (2014) 'BBC Values'. Available from: www.bbc.co.uk/academy/journalism/values/article/art20130702112133786
Hewlett, S. (2011) 'PCC2 can learn a lot about privacy from TV', *British Journalism Review*, 22 (4), pp. 23–25.
Jenkins, S. (2017) 'BBC are "aiding terrorism" says Simon Jenkins', *Newsnight*, 22 March 2017. Available from: www.youtube.com/watch?v=OL9zBNw1Qh8
Linfield, S. (2015) 'Perpetrator Images of Atrocity and Suffering: Then and Now' *in: The Visual Politics of the Human Images in Humanitarian and Human Rights Communication*. London: London School of Economics.
Mahler, J. (2017) 'CNN had a problem, Trump solved it', *New York Times Magazine*, 24 April 2017. Available from: www.nytimes.com/2017/04/04/magazine/cnn-had-a-problem-donald-trump-solved-it.html
Maras, S. (2013) *Objectivity in Journalism*. Cambridge: Polity Press.

McNair, B. (2009) *News and Journalism in the UK*. London: Routledge.

Morrison, D.E. and Svennevig, M. (2007) 'The defence of public interest and the intrusion of privacy journalists and the public', *Journalism*, 8 (1), pp. 44–65.

Ofcom (2016) *The Ofcom Broadcasting Code*. London: Office of Communications. Available from: www.ofcom.org.uk/tv-radio-and-on-demand/broadcast-codes/broadcast-code

Patterson, T.E. (2016) 'News Coverage of the 2016 General Election: How the Press Failed the Voters. Shorenstein Center on Media, Politics and Public Policy'. Available from: https://shorensteincenter.org/news-coverage-2016-general-election/

Phillips, A. (2015) *Journalism in Context. Practice and Theory for the Digital Age*. London: Routledge.

Reuters Institute for the Study of Journalism (2016) 'Editorial Analytics: how news media are developing and using audience data and metrics'. Available from: https://reutersinstitute.politics.ox.ac.uk/sites/default/files/Editorial%20analytics%20-%20how%20news%20media%20are%20developing%20and%20using%20audience%20data%20and%20metrics.pdf

Ruhfus, J. (2017) 'Can investigative journalism survive clickbait and other challenges?' Al Jazeera, 15 April 2017. Available from: www.aljazeera.com/blogs/europe/2017/03/investigative-journalism-survive-clickbait-challenges-170323112601103.html

Self, W. (2014) 'Click away now: how bloodshed in the desert lost its reality', *The Guardian*, 23 December 2014. Available from: www.theguardian.com/news/2014/dec/23/-sp-passive-consumers-pornography-violence

Shepard, A.C. (2003) 'Columbine school shooting: Live television coverage' *in*: Rosenthiel, T. and Mitchell, A.S. (eds) *Thinking Clearly: Cases in Journalistic Decision-making* (pp. 57–81). New York: Columbia University Press.

7   A world of journalism

Introduction

The *Sunday Times* journalist Marie Colvin, killed in the Syrian civil war in 2012, left an indelible legacy of what it is to be a foreign correspondent and set out in passionate terms why it is important to shine a light into the darkest corners of the world. That mission is to speak the truth to power and make a difference by exposing the horrors of war, especially the atrocities that befall civilians (2010). On the face of it, the digital revolution that has created a globally interconnected media environment means it has never been easier to report from distant places. In the years since the emergence of CNN in 1980 more than 100 international broadcast channels have been launched, barriers to entry have tumbled and journalists' monopoly on international reporting has been cast aside. New media players have surfaced to harness the power of user-generated content, citizen journalism and the multitude of social media platforms. It is hard to remember a time over the past decade when a global disaster or faraway conflict was not covered in virtually real-time in one way or another. But the very technology that has ushered in this global revolution has at the same time wrought financial havoc on many 'legacy' news organisations, ironically reducing their ability to cover international news beyond their borders and forcing a fundamental reappraisal of how foreign news is sourced and delivered.

This chapter explores the basic paradox at the heart of international news journalism and examines a series of key questions. Are we in fact witnessing a new form of global journalism, bringing into the twenty-first century Marshall McLuhan's concept of a 'global village' (1964)? Does the proliferation of new broadcasters pose a genuine challenge to the hegemonic dominance of Western broadcasters such as the BBC and CNN International[1] and, with it, dilute the post-colonial, imperialist view of distant nations? Or are we in fact experiencing the opposite of global journalism, in which new broadcasters are the tool or vanity project of foreign governments aimed at exercising 'soft power' and pushing their own political view of the world? And what are the implications for the dominant objectivity paradigm that for so many years has been the guiding principle behind the news coverage of so many mainstream broadcasters? There are, of course, no easy answers to any of these questions; the broadcast news ecology is complex, multi-layered and different channels have different aims. But one simple fact is certain: the past assumption that foreign news is the sole preserve of an all-knowing foreign correspondent is a thing of the past. Foreign news reporting is undergoing a transformation that has not been seen for 150 years.

This chapter begins by charting the development of international reporting, from the earliest days of the foreign correspondent in the Crimean War to the rise in prominence of CNN International and Al Jazeera in each of the Gulf Wars and to the most recent emergence of international networks such as RT,[2] CCTV[3] and France 24. The chapter then looks at the debate pitting proponents of a new 'global journalism' against those focusing on the political economy and arguing that Western power, corporate interests and liberal economics continue to hold sway over international reporting and continue to shape a 'Northern'-dominated news agenda. Subsequent sections in the chapter analyse how the culture and practice of international reporting is changing, whether 'counter-hegemonic' networks (Painter, 2008) have succeeded in challenging the BBC-CNN view of the world, and the attempt by governments such as those of Russia and China to use broadcasting to extend their use of soft power.

From Crimea to the Kremlin

The roots of international journalism can be traced back to the second half of the nineteenth century with the emergence of the mass-printing press and commercialisation of the newspaper industry in the United States and United Kingdom. The first foreign correspondent is generally thought to have been Henry Crabb Robinson, working for *The Times* in Germany and Spain in the first decade of the 1800s (Williams, 2011: 50). By the time of the Crimean War in 1853, William Howard Russell was in place as the first international war correspondent to capture the embarrassing military setbacks of the British troops for readers of *The Times* (Knightley, 2004).[4] During this period, the first international news agencies were springing up – Havas in 1832 and Reuters in 1851 – both relying on carrier pigeons to relay stories before the invention of the telegraph. Once the telegraph was introduced, their ability to distribute stories quickly led to the rapid expansion and dominance of agencies for international reporting. Their work displayed a clipped, fact-based style as reporters were urged to put facts at the top of the story, partly because long messages were expensive and partly because the first 'cables' had a habit of cutting out halfway through and losing material (Maras, 2013: 28). The rise of the agencies had two main unforeseen consequences. Firstly, they played an important role in the development of the Anglo-American objectivity paradigm, setting the tone more widely not only for the factual basis of reporting (sometimes known as 'telegraphic journalism') but also for the 'inverted pyramid' story construction, still seen as one of the hallmarks of objectivity (Porwancher, 2011: 191). Secondly, the agencies were closely linked to the major colonial powers of the time, such as Britain, France and Germany, creating a lasting legacy that can be still detected today. As Williams observes:

> Colonialism not only moulded how international news is gathered, processed and disseminated today, but also had a profound impact on audience expectations of what international news should be.
>
> (Williams, 2011: 46)

Although the news agencies produced what were on the face of it fact-based stories, they were not without national interference and often had uncomfortably close relationships with their respective governments. In fact, until the 1930s the agencies also effectively divided up the world into 'spheres of influence' for international newsgathering in what was a cartel that held until 1937 (ibid: 55). Ultimately the news agency alliance was undermined by the spread of radio and television and as the agencies started to shake off their close links with governments and become more competitive against each other. But the early days of radio were also very much in the shadow of propaganda and narrow national interests. The BBC's international radio station, launched in 1932, was tellingly called The Empire Service. It took World War II and the collapse of the British empire to usher in a more independent editorial stance. It was, for example, not until 1956 during the Suez crisis[5] that the then general manager of Reuters, Christopher Chancellor, ordered journalists, much to the disgust of Sir Anthony Eden's government, to stop referring to British troops as 'our' troops. And while agencies have suffered a series of financial crises in recent history (after two bankruptcies in the 1980s, UPI is a shadow of the news organisation that once competed with the Associated Press), they have remained a major source of international reporting. If anything, reliance by other news organisations on the agencies has increased over the past decade as newspapers systematically cut costs and reduce the number of foreign correspondents to the bare bone.[6]

At the same time as the news agencies were becoming more independent, so too the first of the Western 24-hour news channels started to emerge. When CNN was launched in 1980 it was available to 1.7 million US households via cable. Today, the global arm CNN International is available to two billion people around the world in 200 countries and territories using a wide array of platforms. Soon, other major Western nations followed suit, with an explosion of 24/7 satellite news channels around the globe (Rai & Cottle, 2007: 51). The BBC set up its own BBC World Service Television in 1991, subsequently changing its name and branding to today's BBC World News. By 1996, both Fox News and MSNBC launched their 24-hour news services in the United States to rival CNN. Fox and MSNBC clearly have overt political leanings and are much more dependent on competitive business models than the taxpayer-funded public service BBC. But all these 24-hour channels have one thing in common – their view of international news is rooted in the Anglo-American tradition of journalism that evolved in the nineteenth century and is based on Western social and economic values. Put bluntly, they are accused of broadcasting from 'the West to the rest'. It was frustration at this, and such charges of cultural imperialism, which were partly responsible for the emergence of another wave of new stations whose goal was, at least on the face of it, to challenge this worldview. This new wave of stations has included, amongst more than 100, prominent names such as Al Jazeera (founded in 1996) and Al Arabiya (2003) in the Arab world, Euronews (1993), China's 24-hour-news English language channel as part of the CCTV network (2000), Russia Today (2005), France 24 (2006), Iran's Press TV (2007).

Global journalism or global dominance?

The debate about the role of international news broadcasting in this increasingly crowded and diverse ecology has led to a clear split into two contested arguments (Cottle, 2009: 341) in which the academic debate remains unresolved.

On the one hand, there are proponents of a 'global dominance' paradigm, in which transnational media corporations and Western news agencies, drawing on the long colonial history outlined above and driven by commercial imperatives, seek to capitalise on global deregulated markets. Thussu, for example, argues that although there may be a greater sense of the democratisation of news flows, the dominant players are still Western (2003: 119). This dominance has been strengthened by movements of global capital and by the rise of transnational conglomerates such as News Corporation led by Rupert Murdoch. The Anglo-American news ethos is further supported in television by the fact that just two global agencies – Reuters Television and Associated Press Television News (APTN) – have a virtual duopoly on the supply of wholesale news footage to 24-hour news channels. As Thussu observes, content from Reuters and APTN also comes pre-packaged in ready-to-air format and can be taken straight into a news bulletin without editing (2003: 120). In addition, the news output of BBC and CNN International is monitored widely for breaking news by other 24-hour news channels around the world, playing a major role in agenda-setting according to Western values. Proponents of the global dominance view argue that, despite the digital revolution, UNESCO's 1974 report on the imbalance in international media flows outlining the cultural imperialism and dominance of Western media still holds good today.

On the other hand, there is a 'global public sphere' paradigm, with claims that global satellite news channels are now inventing a new form of international reporting which goes beyond the narrow national perspective and sets aside conventional agenda-setting hierarchies (Volkmer, 1999, 2003). According to this argument, technology has broken down geographic barriers and rolling 24-hour news crosses time zones, reinforcing the concept of a globally interconnected media landscape. In 1997, global audiences tuned in to watch the funeral of Princess Diana; viewers around the world came together on 11 September 2001 to watch live the second hijacked plane fly into the World Trade Center; during the 2003 Gulf War, the presence of Arabic broadcasters and their focus on civilian victims provided an alternative news narrative to the sanitised images of Western missiles being fired by coalition forces against Saddam Hussein's Iraq. These are live experiences shared around the world thanks to satellite broadcasting technology. Indeed, Volkmer argues in her 1999 study of CNN that it is a global platform constructing a global public sphere and new political space. Just a decade later, social media performs the same function from a mobile phone. Berglez concedes that the concept of global journalism is undertheorised (2008: 845), but suggests that it has a distinct epistemology, giving different interpretations of the world. Elaborating on this, he states:

> The national outlook puts the nation-state at the centre of things when framing social reality, while the global outlook instead seeks to understand and explain how economic, political, social and ecological practices, processes and problems in different parts of the world affect each other, are interlocked, or share commonalities.
>
> (Berglez, 2008: 247)

In terms of news, this requires journalistic representation of complex relations that goes beyond local, regional or national preoccupations to bring in a global perspective on a story. In a similar vein, Reese talks about how journalism cannot be fully understood apart from the process of globalisation, its social interconnectedness and the ability to view the world as a single place (2010: 344). He also attempts a definition of this global journalism, saying that it may simply mean that the creators, objects and consumers of news are less likely to share the same nation-state frame of reference (ibid: 348). But he also cautions that the process is by no means universal and that few truly transnational media forms have emerged that have a more supranational than national allegiance. Even the foreign news about big international events is often seen through the national journalistic lens.

This contested debate over global journalism therefore poses the questions as to whether there is such a thing today as a 'global journalist' and, if there is, what values and practice might these journalists share? As Reese asks (ibid: 347), "who qualifies as a 'global journalist' and is this just a new term for 'foreign correspondent'"? The next section of this chapter explores this question before later sections look at claims that the new breed of satellite channels is creating a new form of broadcast news to challenge CNN and the BBC.

Foreign correspondent or global journalist?

Evelyn Waugh gave English-speaking nations an unforgettable depiction of the foreign correspondent in his 1938 novel *Scoop*, dramatising the adventures of the hapless William Boot, complete with his 'cleft sticks'[7] and collapsible canoe. That may have been a satirical, larger-than-life portrayal of the role. But there is no doubting that in the second half of the twentieth century, as newspapers and broadcasters still flourished under the old advertising model, a clear culture developed in real life around the figure of the foreign correspondent, a dashing, stiff-upper-lipped adventurer braving danger to bring back news from distant parts. As Williams remarks (2011: 93), foreign correspondents have themselves often cultivated this image through their memoirs, with colourful stories of dodging bullets in their lone quest for the truth. The role has been based on a clear ethos and values.

The American journalist Marie Colvin, referred to at the beginning of this chapter, epitomised that ethos. She was killed by a Syrian government rocket attack, almost certainly deliberately targeted at her, in the Syrian city of Homs, in a war that has claimed the lives of at least 100 journalists since 2011. And yet foreign correspondents are driven to such distant places. As she herself said in a speech in 2010 to commemorate those journalists who had been killed reporting conflict zones:

> Covering a war means going to places torn by chaos, destruction and death, and trying to bear witness. It means trying to find the truth in a sandstorm of propaganda when armies, tribes or terrorists clash.

It is, then, about bearing witness, holding truth to account and making sense of the world for those back home, based on a common belief that the foreign correspondent has specialist knowledge and can adopt an objective, detached outside view. For television audiences the foreign correspondent, for example the BBC's John Simpson or CNN's Christiane Amanpour, is a familiar face and acts as a 'cultural intermediary' between the story and television viewers (Williams, 2011: 94). Critically, the foreign correspondent has espoused Western values, countered propaganda and upheld the democratic role of a free press. Those are the very values that stem from the nineteenth-century Anglo-American tradition and have tended to perpetuate the Western view of the world. As Starkey observes, they may maintain that they are impartial but beneath the skin such international media representations are infused with the values and perspectives of their paymasters (2007: 127).

But over the past two decades a series of factors have combined to suggest that this version of the foreign correspondent is an endangered species. The experienced British journalist Colin Freeman laments that there are today far more people writing about foreign correspondents than there are actually doing it (2016). The BBC's former Director of News Richard Sambrook poses the blunt question (2010): "Are foreign correspondents redundant?" In the heyday of international journalism, in the decade after World War II, there were more than 2,000 US foreign correspondents working around the world. By the 1970s, the figure had dwindled to just 430 and today few US newspapers or broadcasters maintain a full-time correspondent outside the major cities of London, Moscow and Beijing. The same is true for the European press corps, with hardly any correspondents today based in Africa or Latin America. That long-term decline can be attributed to a number of factors, the first and most alarming of which is the increasing physical risk of the job as journalists become explicit targets. The speed of communications and ubiquity of social media mean that every move of dictators, warlords or drug barons can be reported in real-time. Lindsey Hilsum, Channel 4's International Editor, put it this way:

> The rise of satellite TV has made journalists more of a target, because every dictator, general or rebel commander can see that we are uncovering what they are trying to hide.
>
> (Hilsum, 2012)

Figures collated by the New York-based non-profit organisation The Committee to Protect Journalists (CPJ) show that a shocking 1,236 journalists have been killed since 1992, 48 of them in 2016. Over the past 25 years, the deadliest countries have been Iraq, Syria and the Philippines. Some 26% of these deaths have been of broadcast reporters and a further 16% cameramen and women. A second factor leading to the rapid decline of foreign correspondence has been the collapse of the business model and the competitive pressures that have been referred to throughout this book. The expense of reporting from distant countries has always left international news exposed as the first source of budget cuts, and the logic of Western news values – and audience interest – has left large swathes of the world uncovered, particularly Africa and Asia. The days when foreign correspondents were sent abroad for five years with a generous allowance for housing and schooling for children are fast disappearing. The Shorenstein Center has estimated that the cost of running a foreign bureau (without capital investment) can be up to $300,000 a year once the cost of rent, insurance, 'fixers' and expenses are taken into account. A third and decisive factor is the rise of social media and citizen journalism. The constant flow of such material into newsrooms in major capital cities such as London, Washington and New York has made it easier to dispense with the services of expensive foreign correspondents. Garrick Utley, the late NBC television journalist who had reported from around the world, including the Vietnam War, 1968 Soviet invasion of Czechoslovakia and fall of the Berlin Wall in 1989, had no illusions about the trajectory of international news. "Today and in the future," he wrote presciently in 1998, "anyone sending information from one country to another is a de facto foreign correspondent."

These developments have led to clear consequences. A report in 2010 by the Media Standards Trust in the United Kingdom found that there had been a 40% decline in international news covered by four top newspapers[8] in the period between 1979 and 2009. International news as a percentage of all stories dropped to just 11% from 20% in the same period. Broadcast news has seen a similar trend. A report called *The Great Global Switch-off*, commissioned in 2009 for Oxfam, Polis and the International Broadcasting Trust, concludes that unless urgent action is taken, factual programming about international affairs could be about to disappear from mainstream British television channels. Such news, even in the context of British public-service broadcasting, is being marginalised. Although the BBC and Channel 4 had maintained a level of international reporting, ITV had broadcast just five hours of coverage about the developing world in 2007. As a consequence, despite the global reach of social media, the worldview of television viewers is shrinking rapidly. The report, written by another former BBC Director of News, Phil Harding, concluded:

> When you draw a map of the world, as shown by British factual television, you get a very distorted view. Most programmes are about the US and Europe. The US is largely crime, Europe travel or property. Africa is small and almost entirely about wildlife; South America just about invisible.
>
> (Harding, 2009)

Crucially, the Harding report questions whether international news coverage has moved beyond the parochial level of national interest to explore the truly global dimension, asking:

> Where in this globalised world that is talked about so much are the programmes that make the connections between the different parts of the world and explain how our lives are affected by the actions and decisions taken thousands of miles away?
>
> We hear a lot of talk about a globalised world and the connections across it but it seems much of our television output has yet to fully grasp this important idea.

Part of this reflects the view of commissioning editors and news editors (potentially wrong) that audiences are not interested in foreign news. In equally critical terms, the BBC's foreign correspondent David Loyn, writing a foreword to the Media Standards Trust report, concluded that the state of international reporting may be returning to a world before *The Times*'s William Howard Russell's dispatches from the Crimean War in the 1850s.

Given this irreversible decline, what then comes in its place and does it bear any resemblance to Berglez's concept of global journalism? The new digital media ecology is undoubtedly transforming the nature of foreign reporting, bringing, as explored in Chapter 2, a mixture of opportunity and threat. The provision of instantaneous footage of events through social media, illustrated by virtually live coverage of terror attacks in Paris, London and Brussels, is placing a renewed emphasis on breaking news. With it comes a conviction that news organisations need to place an accent on verifying the authenticity of user-generated content and an increased demand for analysis and contextualisation of news. This has led to an emerging concept of 'curation' as journalists learn to sift through incoming material, select, bundle and package it. This new function has been called 'gatewatching' (Bruns, 2003) as opposed to the traditional journalistic role of 'gatekeeping', allowing material to be used while constantly surveying it for reliability and accuracy. Arguably, this increases transparency, leads to greater diversity of views and can reduce any inherent bias in a news organisation's reporting staff (ibid). But it also illustrates the practical consequence of replacing foreign correspondents with cheaper 'stringers' or freelance journalists, with citizen journalists or user-generated content. Franks argues that this leads to a completely different type and level of coverage and reinforces the 'stay-at-home tendency' of reporting (2005: 97). Sambrook, answering his own rhetorical question about the potential redundancy of foreign correspondents, says they will not disappear altogether, but their role is already changing rapidly, with social media "leading, supplementing and complementing what professional news organisations offer, providing fresh source material for reporters but also competing for public attention" (2010: 2). Foreign reporting, when done in person, is now much more likely to rely on local reporters rather than the traditional male, middle-class correspondent 'parachuted' in from a Western capital or sent on a three- to five-year assignment. That may be expected to add a more diverse perspective to reporting, with the added benefit that local staff have an inherently deeper knowledge of a country's culture (and speak the language, which is not always the case with foreign correspondents). Sambrook argues that foreign news desks need to take a more networked approach to international reporting, drawing on such local staff, user-generated content and freelancers to provide swift analysis of news without the major overhead of a foreign bureau and permanent staff (2010: 101).

But while the role of foreign correspondents and international reporting is changing, there is no sign that Western news executives are about to dilute the underlying ethos and values. Harding is adamant that news organisations have to embrace citizen-based journalism across the world but they must at the same time retain the core values of accuracy and impartiality (2009: 25). Sambrook maintains that news organisations have an absolute responsibility to bear witness (2010: 102).

Challenging the BBC-CNN view of the world

To judge by this, there is little sign that the cultural dominance of the West is on the wane or that a new form of global journalism is being conducted by Western broadcasters in practice. Analysis of the shrinking coverage of foreign news discussed above has shown a clear bias towards the English-speaking world at the expense of Africa and Asia. The Harding report found that 47% of all British public-service broadcasting coverage of international news focuses on North America and Europe. Franks laments that although technological advances allow us to cover the most remote locations, many parts of Africa are less understood and less well reported than they were several generations ago. And as the need to explain the interconnected nature of the world grows, so audiences in the United States and United Kingdom appear to be satisfied with an emphasis on domestic news.

So have any of the new names in the international broadcast news environment succeeded in breaking the dominant BBC-CNN view of the world? Both Al Jazeera and France 24 can lay claim to that.

Al Jazeera, for one, could be expected to take a different view of the world given its Qatari funding base and Arab ownership. The station, both in its original Arabic broadcasting and its English language service, divides opinion amongst politicians and journalists alike. Some maintain that it is biased in favour of the Arab world and dependant on the Qatari royal family; others say it is the voice of the Arab street and offers a different viewpoint from the hegemonic BBC-CNN perspective while at the same time upholding journalistic values of accuracy and fact-based reporting. Certainly, Al Jazeera was able to recruit several reporters who had worked for the BBC Arab Service as the plug was pulled on the latter in 1996. Initially at least the BBC ethos and culture moved across but it was not long before Al Jazeera was dragged into controversy, particularly when after 11 September it broadcast several tapes from the al Qaeda leader Osama bin Laden. Inevitably it became labelled as an apologist for terrorism and propaganda. The station subsequently caused outrage in the United Kingdom and was criticised by prime minister Tony Blair when it broadcast pictures of dead British soldiers during the 2003 Gulf War. During that war, a US missile hit its Baghdad office, killing correspondent Tareq Ayoub and wounding another Al Jazeera journalist. The perspective of Arab suffering during the war came in stark contrast to the first Gulf War in 1991, which had cemented CNN's dominance in 24-hour broadcast news. Then, reporting had been from a strictly Western perspective, often from reporters covering the US military and showing sanitised US official footage of weapon strikes that reminded viewers of video games. The cliché has it that the BBC and CNN show the 'outgoing' missiles, while Al Jazeera shows the consequence of the 'incoming' fire. In addition to that, the network has gained a reputation for showing graphic images of the dead and dying, often zooming in closer on victims than would be normal with mainstream Western news organisations.

Williams argues that Al Jazeera *has* offered a different perspective, with the capacity to envision the emerging world order differently and challenging the dominant perspective of Western media (2011: 75). Al Jazeera does make a point of trying to devote more coverage to the voiceless and the global South, aiming, in its own words, to reach "some of the most unreported places on the planet".[9] It claims to challenge established narratives and give a global audience an alternative voice. Painter concurs, arguing in his study of the English-language service (AJE) that the network is the most interesting development over the past few decades in the attempt to provide news from the South (2008: 12). That is not to say, however, that it has embraced a style of journalism that departs radically from the West's dominant objectivity paradigm. Indeed, it can be argued that it has played a major role in bringing professional journalism standards to the Middle East. The format of its news bulletins, especially in English, resembles that of the BBC and CNN. And in common with many Western news organisations, Al Jazeera publishes its code of ethics on its English-language home page. That code would sit comfortably with many of its Western rivals, stating its determination to "adhere to the journalistic values of honesty, courage, fairness, balance, independence, credibility and diversity, giving no priority to commercial or political over professional consideration".[10] Critics would argue that, despite this, stories about the Qatari royal family are strictly off limits. In the United Kingdom it is subject to Ofcom regulation like other broadcasters, triggering complaints predictably when it reports on issues around the Israeli-Palestinian conflict.[11]

In contrast to Al Jazeera, France 24 is based in the suburbs of Paris, at the heart of the European Union. But there are many similarities. It too was born of the frustration at the BBC-CNN dominant world perspective. It too tends to adopt the typical format of a Western-style 24-hour rolling news channel, espousing the very same values of objectivity and impartiality. And it too seeks to redress the imbalance of global reporting, stating that it offers viewers "comprehensive coverage of world events, with a focus on cultural diversity and contrasting viewpoints via news bulletins, reports, magazines and debates".

It was president Jacques Chirac who highlighted his anger and a feeling in France that the nation had needed greater international presence in the media to put its views across in the build-up to the second Gulf War. In 2002, he relaunched an on-off project that had dated back to 1987, saying:

> The recent crises have shown the handicap that a country suffers, a cultural area, which doesn't possess a sufficient weight in the battle of the images and the airwaves. Let us question, in the time of terrestrial television networks, of satellite, of the internet, on our organisation in this domain, and notably in the dissipation of public funds which are reserved to them.

France 24 finally launched in December 2006, broadcasting on two channels, in French and English. Since 2010 it has also broadcast in Arabic and now has a live stream available on YouTube. Critics say it has not managed to capture audiences in the same way as Al Jazeera has and its programming is viewed as bland. There have been times when it has managed to put across a French political point of view, balancing finely the tension between objectivity and a national perspective. But its stretched budgets mean it has been unable to indulge in comprehensive overseas reporting. Any alternative French perspective and values have been mostly evident in cultural and lifestyle programming (Painter, 2008: 14).

Soft power – back to the future?

In a sense, France 24 is a project born of a government's desire to exert 'soft power' in the world. But other newly launched broadcast channels have taken this concept to new levels. Russia's RT, Iran's Press TV and China's CCTV/CGTN are on the face of it 24-hour rolling news channels but all are vociferous proponents of their respective governments' views. There is no pretence here of covering a global agenda or of upholding Western concepts of balance and impartiality. All three have a strong political agenda and set out to counter the dominant Western narrative. As such, these channels hark back to the propaganda that filled the radio airwaves in the 1930s, the Nazi era and Cold War rivalries between East and West.

These early propaganda vehicles were also rooted in cultural imperialism and designed to spread a specific worldview. Radio Moscow began a shortwave service in 1925, followed by the BBC's Empire Service, after five years of experimental broadcasts, in 1932. When Hitler came to power in 1933, his government quickly harnessed the power of radio and used it throughout World War II, producing seven million cheap radios or Volksempfänger[12] and broadcasting propaganda into Britain. Voice of America (VoA) was launched in 1942, and when the Iron Curtain fell over Eastern Europe Radio Moscow and its satellite stations were pitted against CIA-backed Radio Free Europe and Radio Liberty.

Today, a new generation of state-controlled broadcasters is flexing its muscles, causing concern in Western capitals. In 2011, the then US Secretary of State Hillary Clinton warned the Senate Foreign Relations Committee that the United States was losing an information war at the hands of Arabic news channels and English-language programming from China and Russia.

> During the Cold War, we did a great job in getting America's message out [she said]. After the Berlin Wall fell we said, 'okay, fine, enough of that. We've done it. We're done.' And unfortunately, we are paying a big price for it. And our private media cannot fill that gap.
>
> So, we are in an information war. And we are losing that war. I'll be very blunt in my assessment. Al Jazeera is winning. The Chinese have opened up a global English-language and multi-language television network. The Russians have opened up an English-language network. I've

seen it in a few countries, and it's quite instructive. We are cutting back. The BBC is cutting back.

(Clinton, 2011)

RT, launched in 2005 as Russia Today, broadcasts in Russian, English, Spanish and Arabic and is funded by the Russian state. And most controversially in 2010 it launched RT America, specifically targeting an American audience. The network's channels are widely viewed in the West as representing the voice of President Putin and being an integral part of Russian foreign policy. According to Yablokov, the Kremlin adopted a policy in 2000 of promoting a new image of Russia abroad, paving the way for broadcasting outlets that were intended to stem flows of negative information from the West (2015: 304). The president himself, visiting the station in Moscow in 2013, spelt out very clearly the goal of countering the dominant Western broadcasting perspective, saying:

> When we designed this project back in 2005 we intended introducing another strong player on the international scene, a player that wouldn't just provide an unbiased coverage of the events in Russia but also try, let me stress, I mean – try to break the Anglo-Saxon monopoly on the global information streams.

In contrast to Al Jazeera and France 24, which have tried to redress the imbalance in the dominant Western broadcast perspective, RT has been accused of outright anti-Americanism. It has carved out a specific space in media by reporting on little-known news stories and international scandals involving the US government, stoking conspiracy theories, some of which have been around for decades (Yablokov, 2015: 306). That in turn has allowed it to generate an anti-elitist message and tap into domestic US audiences and play on social and economic inequalities in American society (ibid: 307). President Obama's Secretary of State John Kerry said RT had been more or less full-time devoted to propaganda and distorting what was happening on the ground in the Ukrainian conflict with Russia. There is also strong evidence that RT's correspondents have not been able to carry out their reporting without political interference. In 2008, the young RT correspondent William Dunbar resigned from his position in Georgia covering the conflict with Russia after his stories about a Russian air raid on civilians were cancelled. He wrote of his frustration in *The Independent* newspaper (2010), saying: "The station has some great stories and some talented people. But on any issue where there is a Kremlin line, RT is sure to toe it."

One of RT America's Washington-based news anchors, Liz Wahl, resigned spectacularly on air in 2014 accusing the network of whitewashing Russia's military intervention in Ukraine. She departed from her script, saying:

I cannot be part of a network funded by the Russian government that whitewashes the actions of Putin. I'm proud to be an American and believe in disseminating the truth, and that is why, after this newscast, I'm resigning.

While Western networks had reported that Russian troops had been involved in the campaign, RT kept to the Kremlin line that military forces were made up entirely of local self-defence forces. RT countered that Wahl's action was a self-promotional stunt and that she should have addressed her grievances with the editor. The British regulator has found RT to be in breach of its impartiality rules at least ten times since its launch.

Iran's Press TV was launched in 2007, is state-funded and thought to be close to the country's conservative political faction. Painter describes it as a largely political response by then President Mahmoud Ahmadinejad to a government under siege from the then Bush administration in the United States (2008: 15). It too has adopted the same style of half-hour rolling bulletins so familiar from Western 24-hour news channels but, in the same vein as RT, it is aimed at setting out the Iranian perspective of the world and ending the stranglehold of Western media. In the early years Iran, like Russia, was also able to finance its international broadcasting venture on the back of strong oil revenues as the prices rose during 2008 to over 100 dollars per barrel. But Press TV has rarely been free of controversy, with critics calling it pro-Palestinian, anti-Semitic, anti-American and a propaganda platform for the Iranian government. The British presenter Nick Ferrari quit his show on Press TV in 2009 in protest at biased cover of the Iranian elections which clearly breached Western journalistic norms. "I imagine they've been told what to do," (Fletcher, 2009) Ferrari told *The Times* newspaper, "and I can't reconcile that with working here." Like RT, it has also been accused of running conspiracy-theory stories. Capturing a sense of rising outrage in the United Kingdom, the British journalist and commentator Nick Cohen urged the authorities in an opinion piece in *The Observer* newspaper to close down what he called a 'hate channel':

> Press TV is not just a home for those with exterminationist fantasies about wiping Israel off the map, but a platform for the full fascist conspiracy theory of supernatural Jewish power. Other fantasies follow. The 9/11 attacks on Washington and New York and 7/7 attacks on London were inside jobs, according to its commentators. Plots emanating from Buckingham Palace, and orchestrated by that sinister figure, the Queen, threaten its journalists.
>
> (Cohen, 2011)

The next year Press TV was effectively closed down in the United Kingdom. Ofcom banned the network from broadcasting in the country after it was found to be in breach of the 2003 Communications Act. The breaking point was the discovery by Ofcom that Press TV's editorial operations were run directly from Tehran, a clear breach of its licensing rules in the United Kingdom. The channel hit back at the decision, saying it believed Ofcom to be the media tool of the British government and that the ban was politically motivated. But by 2013, Press TV had also been removed from some satellite platforms in Europe and America as a result of sanctions against Iran.

The third – and by far the largest – of this trio of non-Western broadcasters seeking to exert soft power across the globe is China's CCTV. In marked contrast to RT and Press TV, CCTV has quietly but steadily built up a substantial international broadcasting presence, now generally branded as CGTN, eschewing the others' aggressive and often confrontational tone of reporting. As part of that push to extend Chinese influence, CCTV opened a new multimillion-dollar Washington headquarters in February 2012, having already established an Africa hub in Nairobi. The moves are part of what has been a multibillion-dollar investment in China's state-run media to expand abroad – this has included the official news agency Xinhua, China Radio International and state newspapers *China Daily* and *People's Daily*. They all have three things in common: they are well-known media in their native China, they are government-owned, and they represent the official voice (Si, 2014: 3). Commenting on China's goals of soft power shortly after the launch of CCTV America from the new Washington studios, *Columbia Journalism Review* wrote:

> The Communist Party hopes to remake the negative image of China that it perceives in coverage by Western broadcasters. It hopes to replace the images of urban pollution, self-immolating Tibetan monks, and sweatshop workers with those of its rapidly growing cities and a prosperous new consumer class.

Following its expansion, CCTV's seven international language channels broadcast a free-to-air signal that can be accessed by 1.5 billion viewers outside China in 140 countries (Si, 2014: 5). Its actual audience figures are, however, not available. Most recently, Chinese foreign correspondents have become an ever-increasing presence at big international stories, from the major Western capitals of Washington and London to conflict hotspots in Syria, Iraq and Libya. Today CCTV has 70 bureaux worldwide.

CCTV's global expansion means that it has effectively emulated the organisational structure of Western broadcasters, with its network of foreign correspondents, overseas offices and rolling 24-hour news channels. CCTV has also attempted to counter the assumption that it is purely a mouthpiece of the Chinese state, arguing instead that it represents Chinese culture more generally. To this end, its Washington operation has hired many non-Chinese staff, including some from established US networks (ABC and CNN) and the BBC. But the West has remained sceptical about many aspects of its operations, from its business practices to its editorial values. The BBC has voiced concern that CCTV is posing a direct threat to its own global reach by paying local broadcasters in Africa to take its content. The charge is that CCTV's state-owned deep pockets allow it to buy its way unfairly into wide distribution at a time when the Beijing authorities are selectively blocking BBC broadcasting in China. At the same time, there has been a refusal to accept that CCTV's international operations conform to Western journalistic values. After the launch of CCTV's American channel, the BBC and Voice of America both characterised the expansion as an attempt to increase the Chinese government's international influence. In her analysis of CCTV's international expansion, Si argues that its news *is* becoming more recognised in Asia and Africa but is not widely watched in Europe and North America and still arouses suspicion:

> Those who know of its existence are suspicious and are aware of the close link to the Chinese government. This leads to questions about the degree of media freedom that CCTV enjoys and general doubt in the credibility of its news coverage.
>
> (Si, 2014: 19)

It remains to be seen whether CCTV's international operations can gain the same credibility that Al Jazeera has managed to establish for its reporting and whether it can shake off the suspicions that it is simply a mouthpiece for Beijing's foreign policy.

Conclusion

The landscape of international news broadcasting has changed beyond recognition in the quarter of a century since CNN first relayed fuzzy green-and-black images of the Western bombardment of Baghdad in 1991. Brave journalists still venture into conflict zones in pursuit of the truth, but, as the appalling death toll of foreign correspondents, freelancers and 'fixers' in Syria and Iraq shows, the risks of reporting from faraway places have never been higher. These risks, combined with relentless cost pressures on legacy broadcasters, have led to deep and widespread cuts in original newsgathering in the field. The foreign correspondent no longer has a monopoly on international news. Local reporting and user-generated content from those caught up in conflict and disaster have to an extent filled the gap; the emergence of Arabic broadcasters such as Al Jazeera and Al Arabiya has added to the sanitised footage of 'outgoing' Western missiles the graphic and disturbing consequences of 'incoming' fire on civilian populations. Undoubtedly, the combination of technological innovation, social media content and wave of new 24-hour broadcast channels has shrunk the world still further and is offering viewers and listeners virtually real-time coverage of global events.

But, at the same time, it is hard to argue that the public is better informed. There are few signs that a genuinely global journalism has emerged from this plurality or that the Western-dominated view of the world has been seriously challenged. Despite the availability of such footage and user-generated content from around the world, the actual amount of foreign news coverage is shrinking. And what remains is still clearly focused on the global North at the expense of Africa, Asia and Latin America. The global wholesale television news agencies Reuters and the Associated Press still dominate the supply of professional footage to 24-hour channels. This duopoly, combined with the BBC and CNN, continues to set the tone for the international news agenda and their output is monitored widely in newsrooms across the world. The newly emerging 24-hour broadcasters have not overtly broken out of this mould, typically adopting Western-style rolling news formats. In addition, as the examples of RT, Press TV and CCTV illustrate, many are narrowly focused on their own national perspective, often driven by a government-funded goal of exerting soft power and promoting their own foreign policy. Few, if any, have moved beyond what Reese refers to as the nation-state frame of reference (2010: 348). Al Jazeera comes closest. It has made great strides since its early days when critics labelled it a 'terrorist network'. It espouses Western-style values of objectivity, has developed a reputation for innovative broadcasting formats and does place a clear emphasis on the global South. But it appears to be an exception to the trend and has struggled to shake off concerns about its Qatari ownership, particularly in the United States, where its American network closed less than two and a half years after launch.[13] In the final analysis, the danger is that the proliferation of new broadcasters will replicate the filter bubble of social media and do no more than serve viewers who want to have their own view of the world affirmed and reinforced.

Notes

1 CNN International, which began broadcasting in 1985, is the global arm of the parent company CNN and is responsible for the international network. It had originally targeted American business travellers staying in hotels abroad but became a mainstream news channel with the launch of BBC World News.
2 RT was formerly known as Russia Today and is funded by the Russian government.
3 CCTV is the main state broadcaster in China. Its overseas network is known as CGTN – China Global Television Network.
4 His epitaph in St Paul's Cathedral, London, refers to him as the 'first and greatest' war correspondent.
5 In 1956, the British government of Sir Anthony Eden sent British troops to Egypt after nationalisation of the Suez Canal, jointly owned by Britain and France since its construction in 1869.
6 See 'Foreign correspondent or global journalist?' (p. 131).
7 William Boot set off to cover the war in Ishmaelia with a ton of baggage, a canoe and, famously, a 'cleft stick' to carry his dispatches. For journalists, it has become a lasting symbol of the lengths they will go to in order to bring a story home.
8 The Media Standards Trust conducted a content analysis on *The Guardian*, *The Daily Telegraph*, *The Daily Mirror* and *The Daily Mail*.
9 See: www.aljazeera.com/aboutus/

10 See: www.aljazeera.com/aboutus/2006/11/2008525185733692771.html
11 A 2007 study by Arab Media Watch concluded cover was broadly balanced in terms of giving the Israeli and Palestinian viewpoint.
12 Literally translated 'people's receiver'.
13 Al Jazeera America's evening prime-time viewing figures were a mere 20,000–40,000 and its finances had been severely undermined by the slump in oil prices.

Chapter bibliography

Berglez, P. (2008) 'What is global journalism? Theoretical and empirical conceptualisations', *Journalism Studies*, 9 (6), pp. 845–858.

Bruns, A. (2003) 'Gatewatching, not gatekeeping: Collaborative online news', *Media International Australia Incorporating Culture and Policy*, 107 (1), pp. 31–44.

Clinton, H. (2011) Testimony to Senate Foreign Relations Committee. Available from: www.foreign.senate.gov/hearings/national-security-and-foreign-policy-priorities-in-the-fy-2012-international-affairs-budget

Cohen, N. (2011) 'Who will rid us of hate channels such as Press TV?' *The Guardian*, 4 December 2011. Available from: www.theguardian.com/commentisfree/2011/dec/04/nick-cohen-press-tv-hatred

Colvin, M. (2010) 'Truth at all Costs.' Available from: www.stbrides.com/news/2010/11/truth-at-all-costs.html

Cottle, S. (2009) 'Journalism and globalization' *in:* Wahl-Jorgensen, K. and Hanitzsch, T. (eds) *The Handbook of Journalism Studies*. London: Routledge.

Dunbar, W. (2010) 'They forced me out for telling the truth about Georgia', *The Independent*, 19 September 2010. Available from: www.independent.co.uk/voices/commentators/william-dunbar-they-forced-me-out-for-telling-the-truth-about-georgia-2083870.html

Fletcher, M. (2009) 'Presenter Nick Ferrari quits Iran Press TV over 'bias' after election', *The Times*, 1 July 2009. Available from: www.thetimes.co.uk/article/presenter-nick-ferrari-quits-iran-press-tv-over-bias-after-election-58rrrvntvp7

Franks, S. (2005) 'Lacking a Clear Narrative: Foreign Reporting after the Cold War', *The Political Quarterly*, 76 (s1), pp. 91–101.

Freeman, C. (2016) 'Job wanted, will travel', *British Journalism Review*, 27 (3).

Harding, P. (2009) 'The Great Global Switch-off: international coverage in UK Public Service broadcasting.' Available from: www.lse.ac.uk/media@lse/Polis/Files/globalswitchoff.pdf

Hilsum, L. (2012) 'Syria and the risk of covering conflicts', *The Guardian*, 24 February 2012. Available from: www.theguardian.com/world/2012/feb/24/syria-deaths-conflict-risks

Knightley, P. (2004) *The First Casualty: The War Correspondent as Hero and Myth-Maker from the Crimea to Iraq*. Baltimore, MD: The Johns Hopkins University Press.

Maras, S. (2013) *Objectivity in Journalism*. Cambridge: Polity Press.

McLuhan, M. (1964) *Understanding Media*. Abingdon: Routledge.

Media Standards Trust (2010) 'Shrinking World: the decline of international reporting in the British press.' Available from: http://mediastandardstrust.org/wp-content/uploads/downloads/2010/11/Shrinking-World-FINAL-VERSION.pdf

Painter, J. (2008) *Counter-Hegemonic News: A Case Study of Al-Jazeera English and Telesûr*. Oxford: Reuters Institute for the Study of Journalism.

Porwancher, A. (2011) 'Objectivity's prophet: Adolph S Ochs and the New York Times 1896–1935', *Journalism History*, 36 (4), pp. 186–195.

Rai, M. and Cottle, S. (2007) 'Global mediations: On the changing ecology of satellite television news', *Global Media and Communication*, 3 (1), pp. 51–78.

Reese, S.D. (2010) 'Journalism and globalization', *Sociology Compass*, 4 (6), pp. 344–353.

Sambrook, R. (2010) *Are Foreign Correspondents Redundant? The Changing Face of International News*. Oxford: Reuters Institute for the Study of Journalism.

Si, S. (2014) *Expansion of International Broadcasting*. Working paper, Oxford: Reuters Institute for the Study of Journalism.

Starkey, G. (2007) *Balance and Bias in Journalism: Representation, Regulation and Democracy*. Basingstoke: Palgrave Macmillan.

Thussu, D.K. (2003) 'Live TV and bloodless deaths: war, infotainment and 24/7 news' *in:* Thussu, D.K. and Freedman, D. (eds) *War and the Media, Reporting Conflict 24/7*. London: Sage.

Volkmer, I. (1999) *News in the Global Sphere: A Study of CNN and Its Impact on Global Communication*. Luton: University of Luton Press.

Volkmer, I. (2003) 'The global network society and the global public sphere', *Development*, 46 (1), pp. 9–16.

Williams, K. (2011) *International Journalism*. London: Sage.

Yablokov, I. (2015) 'Conspiracy theories as a Russian public diplomacy tool: the case of Russia Today (RT)', *Politics*, 35 (3–4), pp. 301–315.

Conclusion
Established media, new challenges

Whither – or wither – the future of broadcast journalism?

Throughout this book, using an apposite mix of polemic and practice, the characteristics of broadcast journalism have been discussed, scrutinised and situated in a number of contexts. Its distinctiveness from, and its similarities with, other forms of journalism have been critiqued from a number of perspectives. As much as has been possible, great attention has been paid to ensuring the discussion and the facts which support it are potentially as enduring as is practical, given the relative longevity of a book such as this. Simultaneously, a number of questions have been raised about the future of broadcast journalism, just as it has been recognised that other forms of journalism have been – and are still being – challenged by emerging practices and technologies that at the very least suggest that this is a sector that doesn't stand still for long. It is a sign of the currency and vibrancy of journalism and its broadcast variant that there is still so much to discuss, and it is hoped that the discussion will continue to usefully exercise both practitioners and academics alike, for a long time to come. This conclusion attempts to draw together some common themes, questions and continuing controversies, while also offering some tentative predictions. These are unlikely to provide closure but they might serve to stimulate further discussion and continue to hold some validity in the not too distant future.

Without doubt, the wider media landscape has been undergoing, and will continue to undergo, profound disruption and change. It was rarely static, as the development of the then 'new' technologies of radio and later television disrupted first the monopoly of print and subsequently the duopoly of print and cinema newsreel. Like the town crier, every medium of mass communication has been challenged by the arrival of new methods for the dissemination of news and information, clarification and comment. As the pace of technological advance has quickened, the rate of change has become exponential, leaving some bewildered not only by the new *status quo*, but also by its potential to again become unrecognisable before very long. While the

Hertzian forms of broadcast journalism, transmitted to unseen and untraceable audiences using electromagnetic radio waves, have been durable relative to others, broadcasters are now facing serious challenges if they are to avoid the fate of audience decline that started to damage the viability of the written press almost two decades ago.

Foremost among those challenges are the changing habits of young people, eager to adopt new technology and platforms, even to the extent of swapping out social media tools that have seemingly only just become ubiquitous for newer ones. In effect, they are continuing the time-honoured tradition of carving out for their generation its own distinctiveness from that which went before, as well as valuing the convenience of the small screen in their pocket over the still-cumbersome furniture of the television and the radio set. Whether this generation of young people will simply mature into the media habits of their predecessors as they grow older remains, of course, to be seen as the rituals of domesticity and parenthood begin to prevail over their lifestyles. Then there are the new online-only start-ups, such as BuzzFeed, Breitbart, VICE and so on, each with its own new unique features, and almost inevitably situated at an ever-newer, ever-sharper cutting edge that is itself destined to be blunted by further new arrivals yet to be imagined. Fundamentally, economic models of profit and sustainability that once worked for established media organisations now face the unprecedented challenge of necessary cost-cutting as social media disrupt the business models of the twentieth century and create an economic environment which appears to be more unstable than ever before.

Journalism – that is *all* journalism – now suffers from a lack of original news reporting, as evidenced by 'efficiencies' in both television and radio, such as the 'hubs' identified earlier as distancing newsgathering from its publics and even separating 'live' newsreading from real-time. Under-resourced newsrooms are populated by journalists overcome by a need for speed in a rush to air, leaving little time or appetite for reflection and the synthesising of a considered view of events and paradigms. Increasingly, ethical challenges have to be dealt with in real-time, their dilemmas made only more intense by business pressures and the implications of algorithms and other unintended consequences of technological advance. On the face of it, there have been many newcomers to the television industry, just as it has been converging with relatively new online activity. However, they are often partisan, sometimes state-owned, organs of propaganda that simply add to the problem of the filter bubble and the echo chamber – although exceptions do exist at present, such as Al Jazeera. In radio, expansion has come from entrepreneurs rather than from propagandists, but automation and 'easy' musical content have for economic reasons led to little innovation in journalism – even diminishing its role where ever-loosening regulation allows, such as in the United Kingdom and other markets facing the same deregulating pressures. Only the relative cheapness of the medium, with its imagined pictures and its greater agility in production, offers some hope – given supportive attitudes from governments and regulators – that radio journalism might yet flourish.

Inevitably, it is the public-service broadcasters that have been shielded to some extent and in some countries, although this is far from the case in the United States, where PBS and NPR struggle to build audiences due to their under-resourcing. But the more the print sector is challenged by economic pressures, the louder it calls for the public subsidy of its broadcast rivals to end. Those siren voices, given the right political contexts, can become all the more effective because less-partisan media present a political threat to the power of the propagandists – the non-resident puppet-master proprietors of newspapers who would control from abroad the destiny of a population while sharing none of its eventual fate. Even in broadcasting, because of tightening budgets and a drive to include local voices, foreign news reporting is diminishing, along with the disappearance of the foreign correspondent and a growing reliance on local reporters and UGC. These last two can often bring benefits to the newsfile, offering images and perspectives that would never before have been seen. But there is no escaping the fact that this trend needs to be treated with caution and calls for an increasing emphasis on the verification of third-party material.

Then there is the role of the audience, in the manifestation of change as much as in its response to change. Now active participants in the processes of generating content, much of that new content is of questionable worth. With new freedoms of choice that should increase pluralism and counter the traditional dominance of partisan voices promoting limited perspectives through the press has come easy access to a wilder world of unverified sources and even more sinister motives. Without increased media literacy, and with a marked absence of responsibility in gatekeeping in largely unfettered social media and irresponsible websites, there has developed a fertile ground for the dissemination of rumour, of fakery and of malicious falsehood. Together these represent a real threat to the proper working of democracy where it exists, often already hanging by a thread. The profession of journalism, even with its often ignored codes of practice and, thankfully, in some broadcast environments underpinned by regulation, at least offers some hope of verification before dissemination and of journalists having undergone the kinds of education and training that promote a sense of responsibility and of perspective. To this it is important to add a sense of what is ethical and what is not, what is acceptable and what is not, and what is, in effect, a true representation of a world few individuals within their audiences can experience for themselves.

New platforms will undoubtedly deliver audiences to traditional forms of journalism as their legacy platforms come under pressure. Inevitably both content and practice will evolve. Broadcast journalism, just as broadcast journalists, has therefore an indispensable role to play in this uncertain future. The challenge will be to tread a fine line between innovation and experimentation on the one hand, and the adherence to sound news values and practices on the other. Failure to do so will mean their voices are devalued and simply added to the ever-growing cacophony of that unruly space that is the Internet.

Index

References to tables are shown in **bold** and to figures in *italics*.